This book belongs to

mackinley

Draw a picture of yourself

Color us in!

Megadoodle

DOODLE and DISCOVER a world of FASCINATING FACTS

DK | Penguin Random House

Edited by Elizabeth Yeates
Additional design by Alison Shackleton
Managing editor Penny Smith
Managing art editor Marianne Markham
Pre-production producer Andy Hilliard
Senior producer Stephanie McConnell
Special sales creative project manager
Alison Donovan

First American edition, 2015

First published in the United States in 2014 by DK Publishing
345 Hudson Street, New York, New York 10014

Material previously published as:
Doodlepedia (2012), Wow (2012), Animal Antics (2013), and Dinosaurs (2013)

Copyright © 2012, 2013, 2014, 2015
Dorling Kindersley Limited
A Penguin Random House Company

15 16 17 18 19 10 9 8 7 6 5 4 3 2
003—269415—May/15

A catalog record for this book is available from
the Library of Congress.

ISBN: 978-1-4654-3433-3

DK books are available at special discounts when purchased in bulk
for sales promotions, premiums, fund-raising, or educational use.
For details contact: DK Publishing Special Markets, 345 Hudson
Street, New York, New York 10014 or SpecialSales@dk.com.

Printed in China

All images © Dorling Kindersley Limited
For further information see: **www.dkimages.com**

A WORLD OF IDEAS:
SEE ALL THERE IS TO KNOW

DRAW A LOOPING, DIVING,
HAIR-RAISING RIDE FOR
THRILL-SEEKERS

DESIGN AN UNBEATABLE,
SWASH-BUCKLING PIRATE SHIP
AND ITS FEARSOME CREW

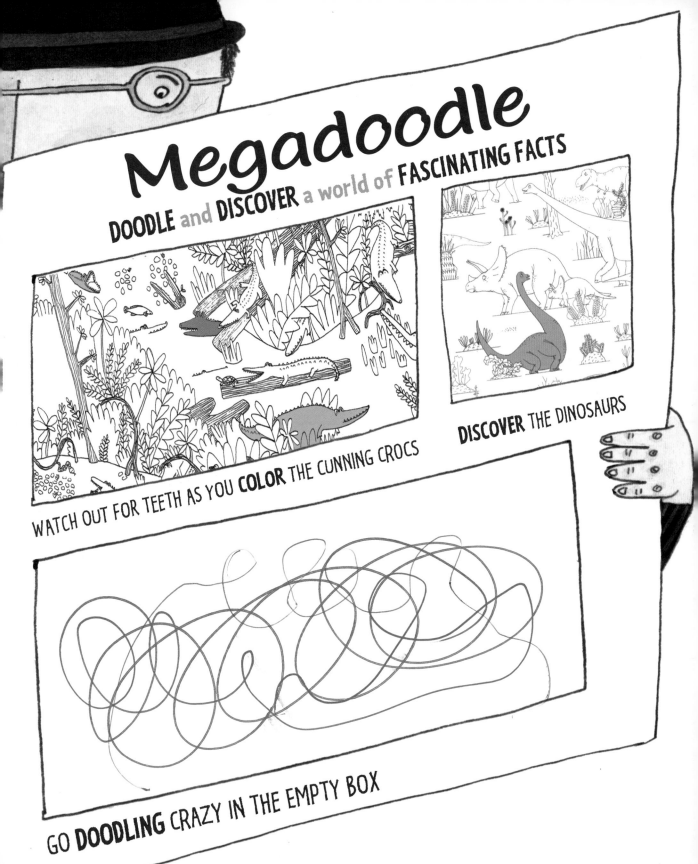

Megadoodle

DOODLE and **DISCOVER** a world of **FASCINATING FACTS**

WATCH OUT FOR TEETH AS YOU **COLOR** THE CUNNING CROCS

DISCOVER THE DINOSAURS

GO **DOODLING** CRAZY IN THE EMPTY BOX

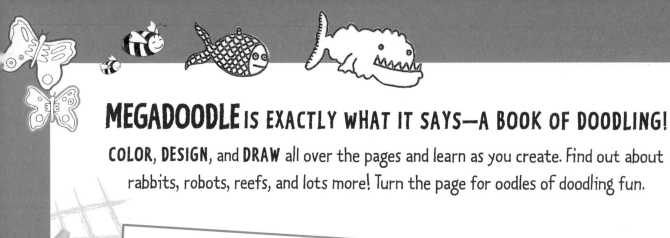

MEGADOODLE IS EXACTLY WHAT IT SAYS—A BOOK OF DOODLING!

COLOR, DESIGN, and DRAW all over the pages and learn as you create. Find out about rabbits, robots, reefs, and lots more! Turn the page for oodles of doodling fun.

DRAW your own futuristic robot

DESIGN scary-looking dinosaurs ready for their dinner

DISCOVER animals that live in the ocean

LEARN about agile spider monkeys

COLOR in the naughty monkeys

DOODLEPEDIA

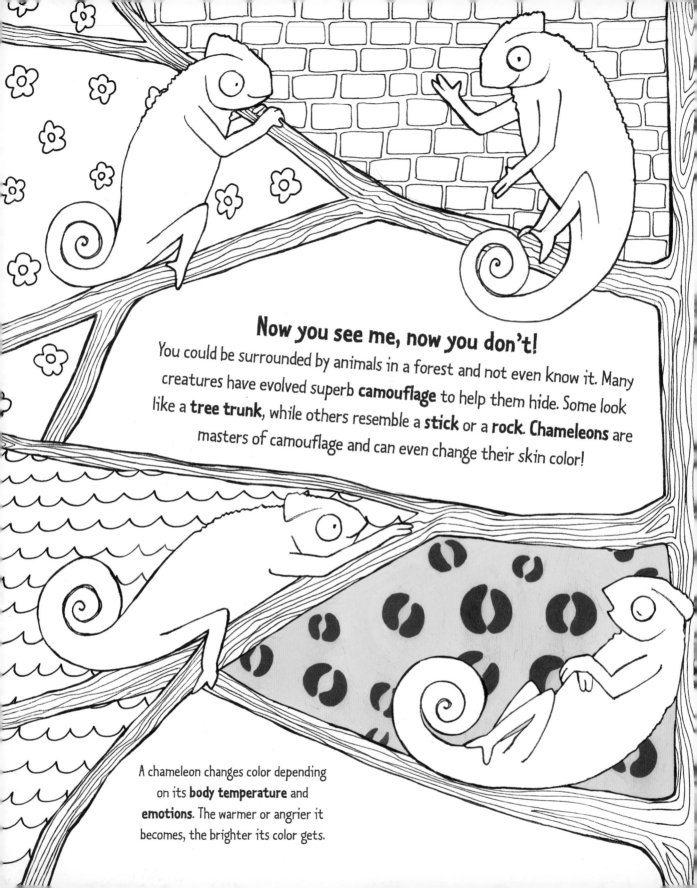

Now you see me, now you don't!

You could be surrounded by animals in a forest and not even know it. Many creatures have evolved superb **camouflage** to help them hide. Some look like a **tree trunk**, while others resemble a **stick** or a **rock**. **Chameleons** are masters of camouflage and can even change their skin color!

A chameleon changes color depending on its **body temperature** and **emotions**. The warmer or angrier it becomes, the brighter its color gets.

Who are you looking at?

You are able to check your **reflection** in the mirror because light bounces off the glass and into your eyes, which send signals to your brain. If a surface is rough, the light **scatters** in different directions, but if the surface is **smooth** and **flat**, the light bounces off at the **same angle** as it enters, creating a reflection.

Light is the fastest thing in the Universe. It travels at about 670 million mph (1 billion kph). It's so fast, it could travel around the world **seven times** in one second!

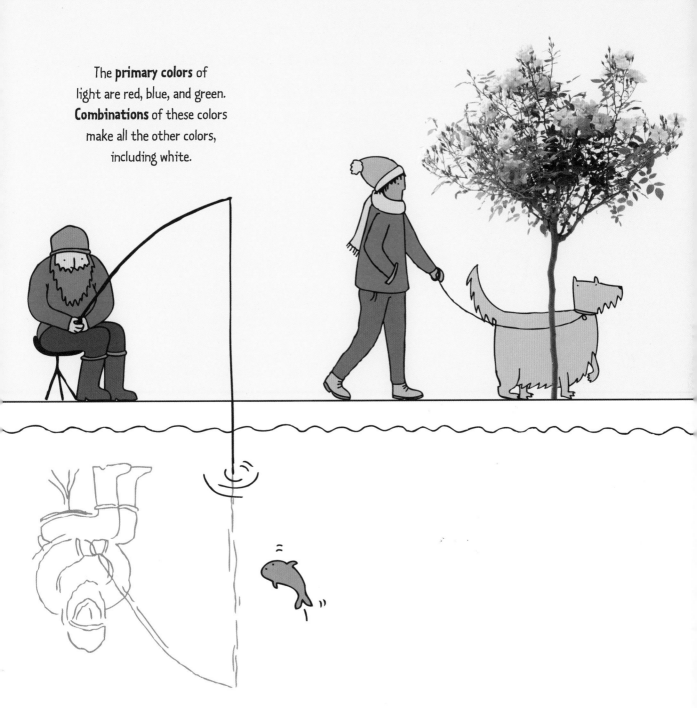

The **primary colors** of light are red, blue, and green. **Combinations** of these colors make all the other colors, including white.

DRAW THE REFLECTION OF EVERYTHING ON THE RIVERBANK

DRAW YOUR OWN TV SHOWS

Channel-surfing craziness!
So many channels and so little time. But before cable TV, there were only a few channels and the picture was **black-and-white!** It wasn't until the **1960s** that the **color television set** first appeared in living rooms around the world.

The TV was so successful that by 1994 **99 percent** of **Americans** home had a **television set**!

COLOR ALL THE VELOCIRAPTOR DRAWINGS YELLOW

Velociraptor

COLOR ALL THE BRACHIOSAURUS DRAWINGS BLUE

Brachiosaurus

Charonosaurus

COLOR ALL THE CHARONOSAURUS DRAWINGS RED

The **Brachiosaurus** weighed up to **55 tons (50 metric tons).** That's the same as **11 African elephants!**

COLOR ALL THE TRICERATOPS DRAWINGS ORANGE

Triceratops

Dino friends

You may have heard about the ferocious **Tyrannosaurus rex**, but can you name more dinosaurs? Dinosaurs came in all shapes and sizes. Some were giant creatures, such as the plant-eating, long-necked **Brachiosaurus**. Others looked really menacing, such as **Triceratops**, but its horny head was used more for defense rather than attack. Speaking of heads, **Charonosaurus** had a long head crest that was used by the males to attract a mate. Not all dinosaurs were big. **Velociraptor** was a waist-high predator with very sharp claws on the back of its feet!

COLOR ALL THE T-REX DRAWINGS GREEN

Tyrannosaurus rex

The Sun

Venus

Earth

Mercury

Mars

Where in the world are we?

Our **solar system** is enormous. Too big even to imagine! It consists of eight **planets**, plus asteroids, moons, dust... the list is almost endless! Everything in our solar system **orbits** around the Sun at different speeds. It takes Earth 365 days to orbit the Sun once, but it takes Neptune nearly 165 years!

The **Sun** is not a planet, but a big, bright **star** situated in the center of the solar system.

Earth's distance from the Sun means it is neither **too hot**, nor **too cold**. It is the only planet suitable for life (that we know of for now)!

DRAW A RANGE OF EXPRESSIONS AND FEELINGS

MAKE ME **HAPPY!**

Face your feelings!

How are you feeling at the moment? Your **facial expression** will probably reveal your current **emotion**. There are many different facial expressions, maybe as many as 5,000! They can be subtle, obvious, and change in an instant. The five key muscles in your face **move** in various directions to turn what you are feeling into an expression.

Fear makes your eyes **widen** to show the whites of your eyes, whereas **anger** makes your eyes become **narrow** and glaring.

MAKE ME **ANGRY!**

MAKE ME **SAD!**

DRAW YOUR OWN MIND-BOGGLING INVENTIONS

The development of the **internal combustion engine** in 1859 changed transportation forever. The burning of **fuel** in an engine made travel much quicker.

Eureka!

From wheels to computers, **inventions** continue to change the way we live. Inventors are always trying to improve an invention already in existence, or thinking of something **completely new**. So the next time you wish there were an invention to help you with your homework or chores, write it down—you could be on to something!

Moles are one of the best diggers in the animal kingdom. Their big, spade-shaped feet make burrowing a swift job.

Hoppy times!

Watch out for that hole! It could be the entrance to a rabbit **warren**, which leads to an underground maze of **tunnels**. Rabbits **excavate** (dig) the long tunnels using their strong legs. By digging underground homes, they provide a safe place for rabbit babies (kittens) to be born.

Foxes are also good diggers and live in **dens.** They sometimes use an empty rabbit burrow to settle down in.

DRAW MORE UNDERGROUND ANIMALS

Doodle gallery!

Art has been around for thousands of years, from cave paintings to modern-day graffiti art. Art is created to record a moment in time, entertain, and to generate an **emotion**, whether it's happiness, fear, or even anger. Art doesn't just have to be a painting—sculptures, collages, and photographs can all be **works of art**.

DRAW YOUR OWN STATUE ON THE PLINTH

Artists can use colours to symbolize a specific emotion. **Yellow** can mean **happiness**, **red** can show **anger**, and **blue** can symbolize **peace** and **calm**.

DRAW YOUR OWN MASTERPIECES IN THESE FRAMES

The **Smithsonian Institution** in Washington DC, America, is the world's largest **museum complex**. There are 19 museums in the complex, with over 135 million pieces of art.

DRAW YOUR OWN WESTERN **MOVIE SCENE**...

The first Western was a **silent movie** made in 1903 called *The Great Train Robbery*.

WANTED

DRAW YOUR OWN WESTERN WANTED POSTER...

Quick on the draw!

A **Western** movie is set in the American Old West (1850s–1900s). A classic Western features a lone **cowboy** fighting for justice, who manages to save a damsel in distress along the way. There is often action in a **frontier town**, with a saloon, bank (good for robbing), and jailhouse (where the sheriff rules).

COLOR THE LIGHTS THAT ARE **POWERED** BY THE **ELECTRIC CIRCUIT**

High voltage!

Electricity is very useful and very dangerous! It's essentially a flow of electrons (miniscule particles). These jump from one atom (a tiny piece of matter) to another. This creates an **electrical current**. **Batteries** contain lots of electrons. When a wire connects the "+" to the "-" terminal on a battery, an electric circuit is made. Break the circuit and you lose power!

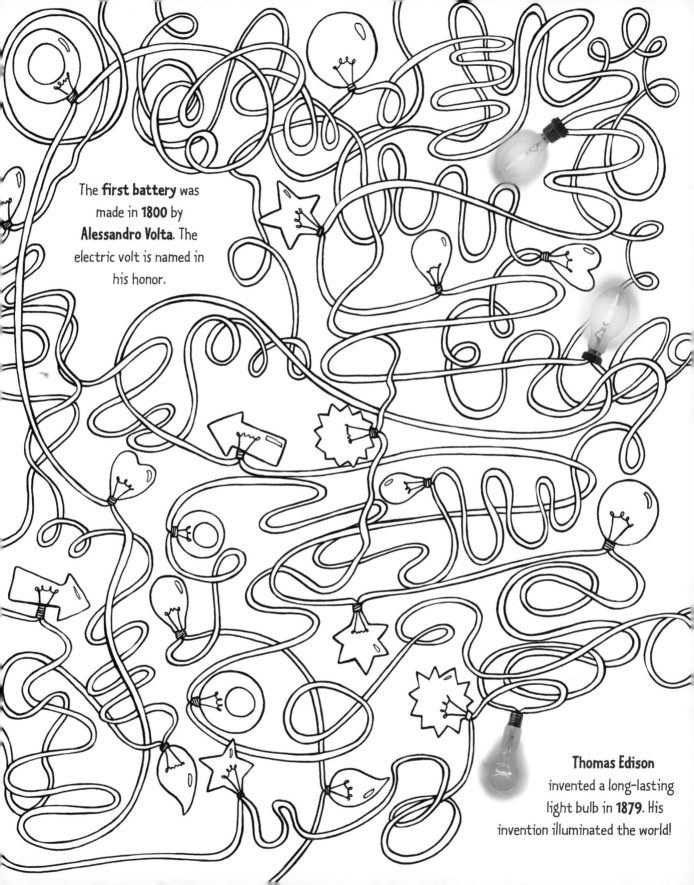

The **first battery** was made in **1800** by **Alessandro Volta**. The electric volt is named in his honor.

Thomas Edison invented a long-lasting light bulb in **1879**. His invention illuminated the world!

Not-so-funny bones

Without bones, humans and animals would be like jello—wobbly and floppy. The **skeleton** allows us to move around and keeps everything inside the body in place. Bones are made up of **living cells**, which help them to **grow** and to **heal** if any of them get broken.

An **adult** human's **skeleton** is made up of 206 bones.

DRAW THE SKELETONS OF THESE ANIMALS

An **elephant's skeleton** consists of more than 300 bones. Elephants don't have any bones in their trunks though, only **muscles**.

Spring ahoy
You are on the side of the Earth that is tilting toward the Sun. Birds nest, grass grows, and the **first flowers** start to **bloom!**

Summertime
Now you are tilted as far **toward** the **Sun** as you'll be all year. All the trees are green and glossy, chicks **fly the nest**, and there are bugs galore.

FINISH **DRAWING** THE DIFFERENT **SEASONS**...

What season it is depends on one thing—if you are **tilted toward or away** from the Sun. As Earth **spins** around its tilted axis, on its **yearly orbit** of the Sun, some regions of Earth tilt toward the hot Sun while others tilt away.

Fall colors

The side of the Earth you are on is tilting **away** from the **Sun**. Leaves on trees turn red, orange, and brown, and it gets **dark earlier**.

Winter chill

You are now **tilted** away from the **Sun** so there's **less sunlight**. It is getting colder, so animals and insects **hibernate**.

Around the middle of Earth is an **imaginary line** called the **equator**, which stays roughly the same distance from the Sun all year round. **Countries** along the **equator** don't have four seasons—just a **dry season** and a **wet season**.

DRAW YOUR OWN GHOULISH MOVIE SCENE...

The first horror movie was made in France in 1896 and was called **Le Manoir du Diable (The House of the Devil)**. This **silent short film** was only three minutes long.

Shock! Horror!
Horror movies feature plots and characters intended to **scare** the life out of the audience. They make people's **worst nightmares** come true! Although horror movies deal mostly with the **supernatural** (monsters and zombies, for instance), they can also feature **baddies** on the loose or an **outbreak** of a deadly disease. Remember to check under the bed at night...

All aboard!

People have been traveling by **train** since 1825, when the **first public railroad** was opened between Stockton and Darlington in the UK. The **track** was just 27 miles (43 km) long. Early trains were powered by a **steam engine**, which was fueled by **burning coal**. Today, trains are powered by **electricity**.

COMPLETE THE TRACK
AND GET THE TRAIN TO THE SEA

FINISH DRAWING THE TRAIN TRACKS

The **longest** train journey in the world is on the **Trans-Siberian Railway** in Russia. The route is 5,752 miles (9,258 km) long and takes seven days.

Twister hysteria!

A **tornado** (also known as a **twister**) is a powerful wind that can wreak havoc. During a **supercell thunderstorm** (when hot, moist air meets cold, dry air), a fast rotating **column of air** can form, extending the storm cloud down to the ground.

Tornadoes can occur anywhere, but they are most common in the Midwestern United States, in an area called **Tornado Alley**.

A tornado's **wind speed** can reach more than 300 mph (480 kph), and it can pick up anything in its path.

DRAW WHAT THE TORNADO HAS SWEPT UP

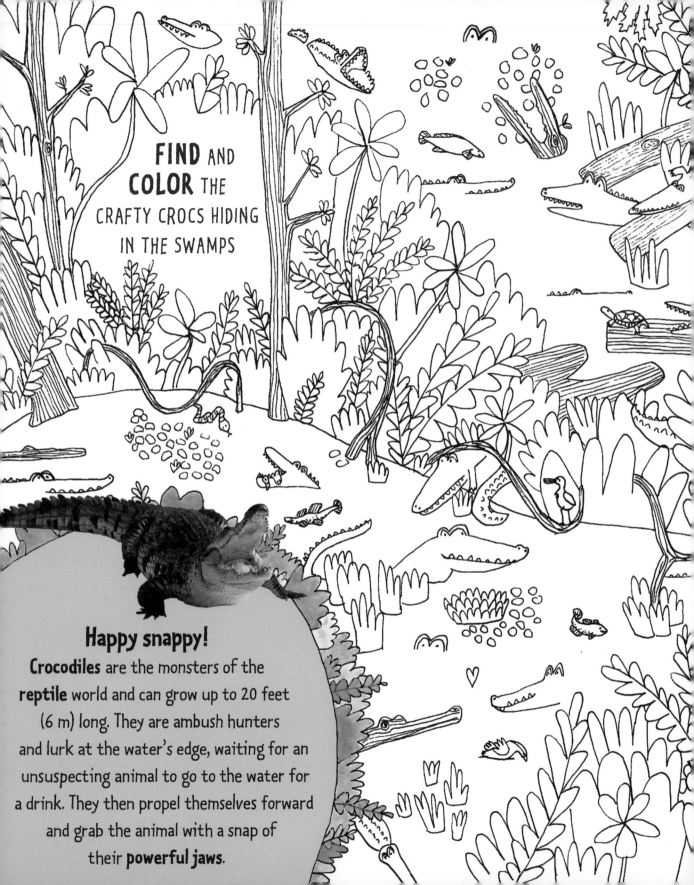

FIND AND **COLOR** THE CRAFTY CROCS HIDING IN THE SWAMPS

Happy snappy!
Crocodiles are the monsters of the **reptile** world and can grow up to 20 feet (6 m) long. They are ambush hunters and lurk at the water's edge, waiting for an unsuspecting animal to go to the water for a drink. They then propel themselves forward and grab the animal with a snap of their **powerful jaws**.

Crocodiles are **carnivores** (meat-eaters) and their diet includes fish, birds, and mammals. Big mammals on the croc menu include zebras, young hippos, big cats, and, very occasionally, people!

Women were often considered bad luck on pirate ships, so they had to **dress up as men** to be allowed to climb aboard.

FINISH THE PIRATE SHIP AND **DRAW** YOUR OWN PIRATE CREW

Blackbeard was a particularly frightening pirate, with his **wild eyes** and **tangled** black beard. He terrorized the seas from 1716–1718.

A pirate's life for me!

Ahoy! Walk the plank! **Pirates** are robbers who travel by sea, and they have been around since ancient times. Long ago, pirates found **riches** galore by stealing gold and gems from **Spanish galleons**. Pirates had fearsome reputations, and they advertised this by flying gruesome **flags** high on the masts of their ships. Gar ha ha!

DRAW THE SHARK'S DINNER **INSIDE** ITS BIG **BELLY**...

·6D S4ARK·

A shark never needs to visit the **dentist** because if it **loses a front tooth** or two, a tooth from the **row** behind moves **forward** to fill the gap!

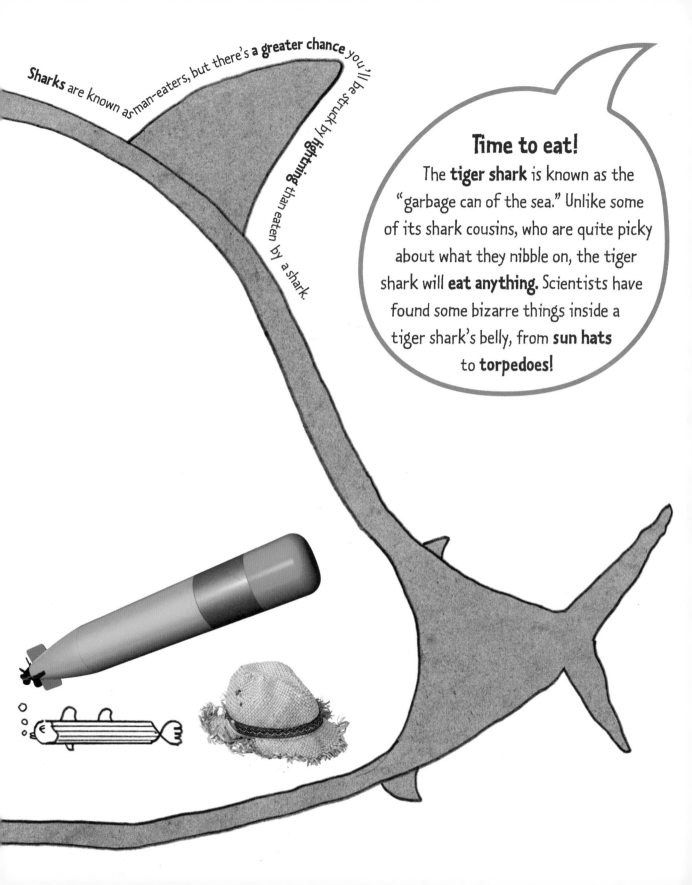

Sharks are known as man-eaters, but there's **a greater chance** you'll be struck by lightning than eaten by a shark.

Time to eat!
The **tiger shark** is known as the "garbage can of the sea." Unlike some of its shark cousins, who are quite picky about what they nibble on, the tiger shark will **eat anything.** Scientists have found some bizarre things inside a tiger shark's belly, from **sun hats** to **torpedoes!**

Hold on tight!

The exciting (and scary) feeling you get when you are on a roller coaster is caused by **G-force**. As you zoom around the roller coaster, G-force acts on every part of your body, even the organs inside you! The G-force on most roller coasters is up to 4.5 g. A top fighter pilot has to contend with 9 g when performing rapid maneuvers, and a scientist once survived a rocket-powered sled ride with a G-force of 46.2 g!

START

At the top of dips the G-force you experience is known as **negative G-force**, and it makes you feel weightless.

START

BIG DIPPER

DESIGN YOUR OWN STOMACH-CHURNING ROLLER COASTER

FINISH

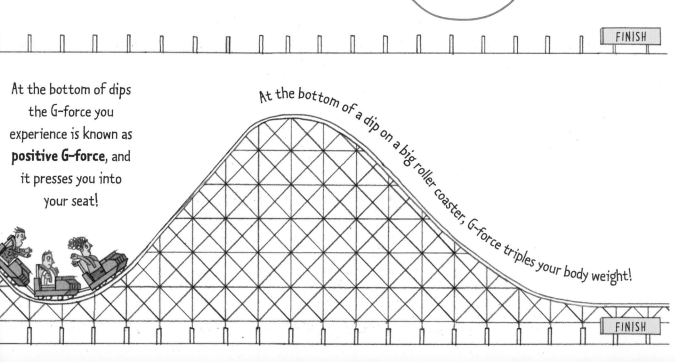

At the bottom of dips the G-force you experience is known as **positive G-force**, and it presses you into your seat!

At the bottom of a dip on a big roller coaster, G-force triples your body weight!

FINISH

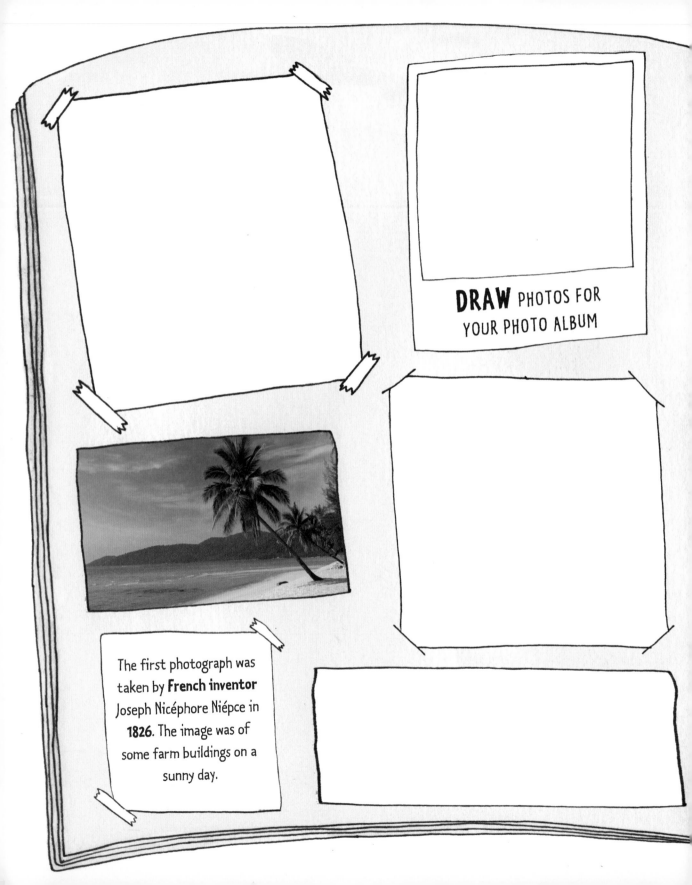

DRAW PHOTOS FOR YOUR PHOTO ALBUM

The first photograph was taken by **French inventor** Joseph Nicéphore Niépce in **1826**. The image was of some farm buildings on a sunny day.

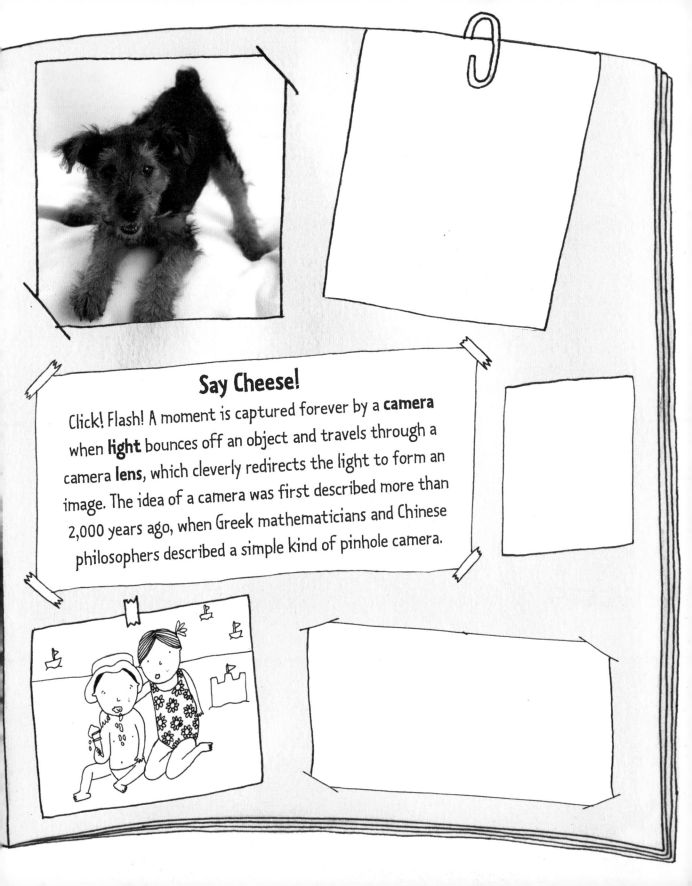

Say Cheese!

Click! Flash! A moment is captured forever by a **camera** when **light** bounces off an object and travels through a camera **lens**, which cleverly redirects the light to form an image. The idea of a camera was first described more than 2,000 years ago, when Greek mathematicians and Chinese philosophers described a simple kind of pinhole camera.

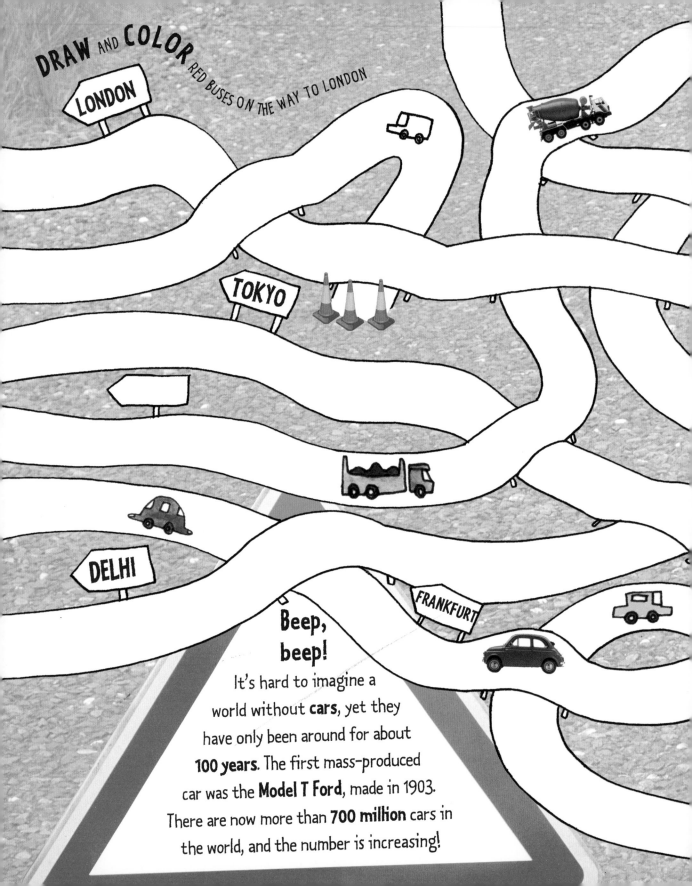

DRAW AND **COLOR** RED BUSES ON THE WAY TO LONDON

LONDON

TOKYO

DELHI

FRANKFURT

Beep, beep!

It's hard to imagine a world without **cars**, yet they have only been around for about **100 years**. The first mass-produced car was the **Model T Ford**, made in 1903. There are now more than **700 million** cars in the world, and the number is increasing!

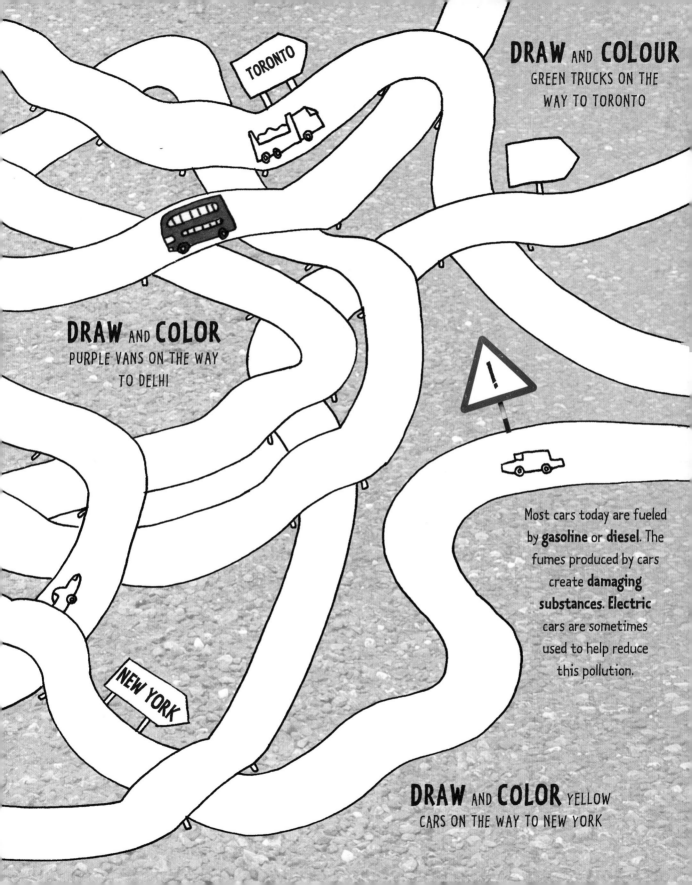

DRAW AND **COLOUR**
GREEN TRUCKS ON THE
WAY TO TORONTO

TORONTO

DRAW AND **COLOR**
PURPLE VANS ON THE WAY
TO DELHI

Most cars today are fueled
by **gasoline** or **diesel**. The
fumes produced by cars
create **damaging
substances. Electric**
cars are sometimes
used to help reduce
this pollution.

NEW YORK

DRAW AND **COLOR** YELLOW
CARS ON THE WAY TO NEW YORK

Hungry plants!

Plants that chomp on insects? Yes, we **carnivorous plants** trap and eat yummy insects and other creepy crawlies. Carnivorous plants can be **passive**, attracting prey that get stuck in **sticky sap** or drown in **pitchers**. Or we can be **active** and actually move to catch our prey. Gotcha!

One deadly plant, **Nepenthes rajah**, is native to the mountains of Borneo. It is so big that it can **take on rats** and **frogs**.

DRAW YOUR OWN BUG-EATING MONSTER PLANT

The **Venus flytrap** is an active carnivorous plant. It has little **hairs** on its padlike leaves that sense when an insect has landed. The hairs prompt the trap to **shut tightly**.

Space to live!
The **International Space Station** (ISS) is made up of lots of modules joined together and it is as big as a **football field**. Up to six astronauts can live there at once, from any of the **16 countries** that helped to build the station. It travels around the Earth at an average speed of **17,210 mph (27,700 kph)**, completing 16 orbits per day!

People have **lived** on the International Space Station **every day** since the **year 2000!**

DESIGN AND **DRAW** YOUR OWN **SPACE STATION**

Digging for diamonds!

Diamonds are **gemstones** and are very valuable. They form deep below Earth's surface and are made from **carbon**. Diamonds are judged according to the four Cs—**carat** (weight), **clarity**, **color**, and **cut**. The bigger, clearer, and more sparkly they are, the more expensive diamonds become!

Natural diamonds are mined from the ground and can take millions of years to form.

They are then cut, using special tools, from a rough stone into a beautiful gem.

Once they are highly polished and sparkly, the diamonds are turned into jewelry.

DRAW YOUR OWN TWINKLING JEWELRY

Hello from up here!

The **North Pole** is in the **Arctic**, which is a frozen area of sea at the **top** of the Earth. Polar bears and killer whales can be found in the Arctic. In December, it is **winter**, and the North Pole is dark all day. In June, it is the Arctic summer, and it is **daylight** the entire time—even at night!

NORTH POLE

DRAW MORE POLAR BEARS LOOKING FOR THEIR DINNERS

NORTH

Hello from down here!

The **South Pole** is in **Antarctica** and is the coldest place on Earth.
Antarctica is a **frozen mountainous continent**, surrounded by ocean,
at the **bottom** of the Earth. Penguins and seals live in this frozen land.
The Antarctic **winter** is in June, and its **summer** is in December.

DRAW MORE PENGUINS HAVING FUN

SOUTH

SOUTH POLE

The shape of things!

Shapes make up our world. Whether it's bicycle wheels (**circles**), a beach towel (**rectangle**), or honeycombs (**hexagons**), everything is made of shapes! Shapes help us build things safely, they allow us to draw fantastic masterpieces, and scientists use them to understand nature!

COLOR THE **OCTAGON** TOWELS **GREEN** AND THE **CIRCLE** TOWELS **BLUE**

octagon (8 sides)

COLOR THE **SQUARE** TOWELS **RED**

DRAW A SPOTTED PATTERN ON THE **TRIANGLE** TOWELS

triangle (3 sides)

Squares are very neat. They have four **sides** of the **same length**. Also, a square's **corners** are all **right angles**—90 degrees. When you add up all the angles they equal 360, which is the number of degrees in a circle!

DRAW SUNBATHERS ON THE **RECTANGLE** TOWELS

square (4 sides)

rectangle
(4 sides)

dodecagon (12 sides)

DECORATE THE **HEXAGON** UMBRELLAS

hexagon
(6 sides)

MAKE THE **DODECAGON** TOWELS STRIPED

COLOR THE **DECAGON** TOWELS **PURPLE**

pentagon
(5 sides)

decagon (10 sides)

DRAW A STARFISH ON THE **PENTAGON** TOWELS

DESIGN YOUR OWN SECURE CASTLE TO KEEP THE ENEMY AT BAY

Castles were built for defense. They had **arrow slits** in the walls so archers could safely shoot arrows at the attackers. The gaps at the tops of the walls, called **crenellations**, made it possible for the defenders to drop heavy stones on the enemy below.

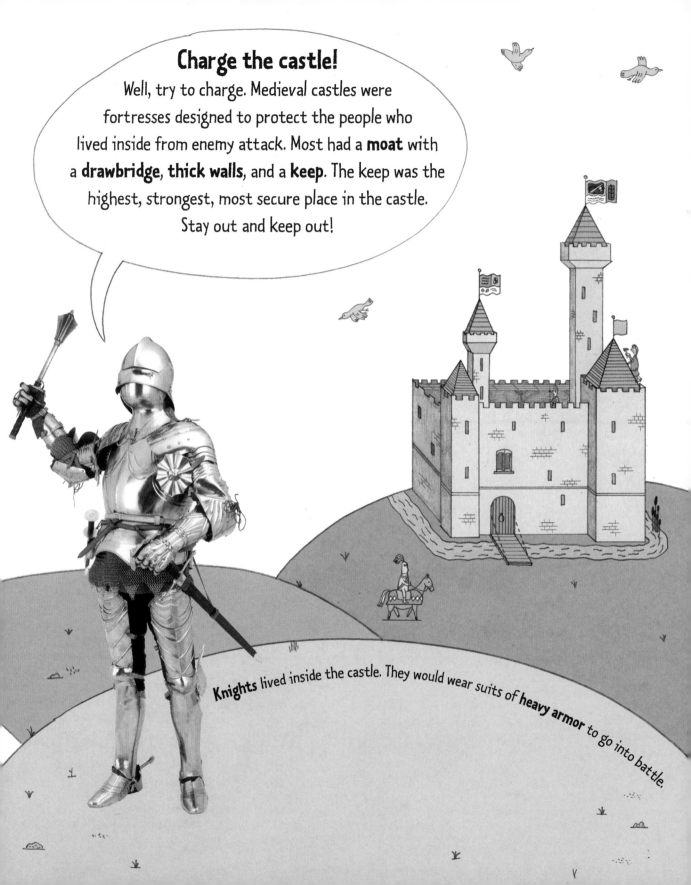

Charge the castle!
Well, try to charge. Medieval castles were fortresses designed to protect the people who lived inside from enemy attack. Most had a **moat** with a **drawbridge**, **thick walls**, and a **keep**. The keep was the highest, strongest, most secure place in the castle. Stay out and keep out!

Knights lived inside the castle. They would wear suits of **heavy armor** to go into battle.

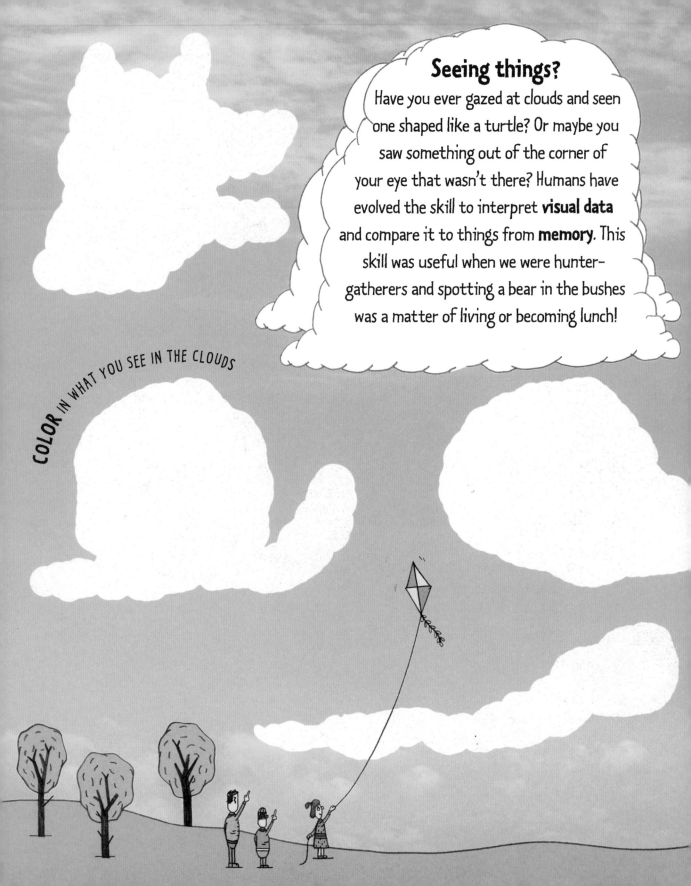

Seeing things?

Have you ever gazed at clouds and seen one shaped like a turtle? Or maybe you saw something out of the corner of your eye that wasn't there? Humans have evolved the skill to interpret **visual data** and compare it to things from **memory**. This skill was useful when we were hunter-gatherers and spotting a bear in the bushes was a matter of living or becoming lunch!

COLOR IN WHAT YOU SEE IN THE CLOUDS

The part of the brain where these visual conclusions are made is called the **ventral fusiform cortex**, also known as the fusiform face area.

Octopuses found in coral reefs live in **dens**. When they feel threatened, octopuses squirt **black ink** to confuse the predator, giving the octopus time to escape.

The world's **largest** coral reef is the **Great Barrier Reef** off the east coast of Australia. It's so big that it can be seen from outer space!

Under the sea!

Called the "rain forests of the sea," **coral reefs** are found under water and are home to millions of marine animals, including fish, turtles, and sea snakes. Although coral looks like a plant or rock, it is actually made up of tiny animals, called **polyps**.

DRAW AND COLOR THE BEAUTIFUL CORAL REEF AND ITS INHABITANTS

A web of flies!

Spiders spin **webs** with one thing in mind—to catch dinner! A spider's web is made from **silk** produced from a spider's **spinneret glands**. A spider will weave its sticky web and wait for its prey to become entangled. Once something is trapped, the spider will rush over and **wrap it up tightly**, ready to eat later.

DRAW WHAT THE SPIDER HAS CAUGHT ON ITS WEB

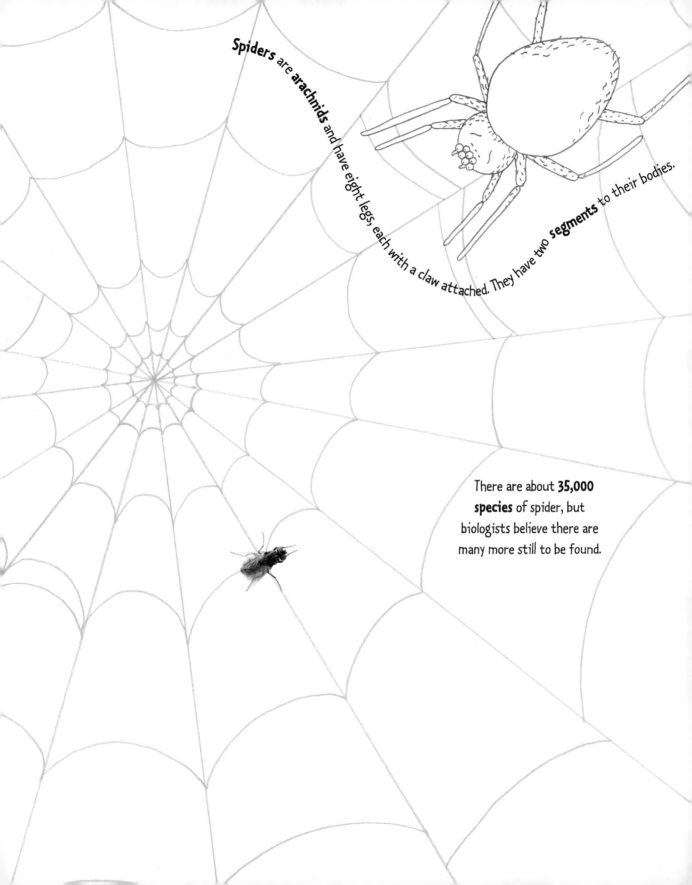

Spiders are **arachnids** and have eight legs, each with a claw attached. They have two **segments** to their bodies.

There are about **35,000 species** of spider, but biologists believe there are many more still to be found.

Blowing your top!

Volcanoes are openings in Earth's rocky crust where **molten rock** bursts and explodes out, or erupts. In addition to spewing out molten rock called **lava**, some volcanoes also blow out huge clouds of **ash** and throw out large, round rocks called bombs.

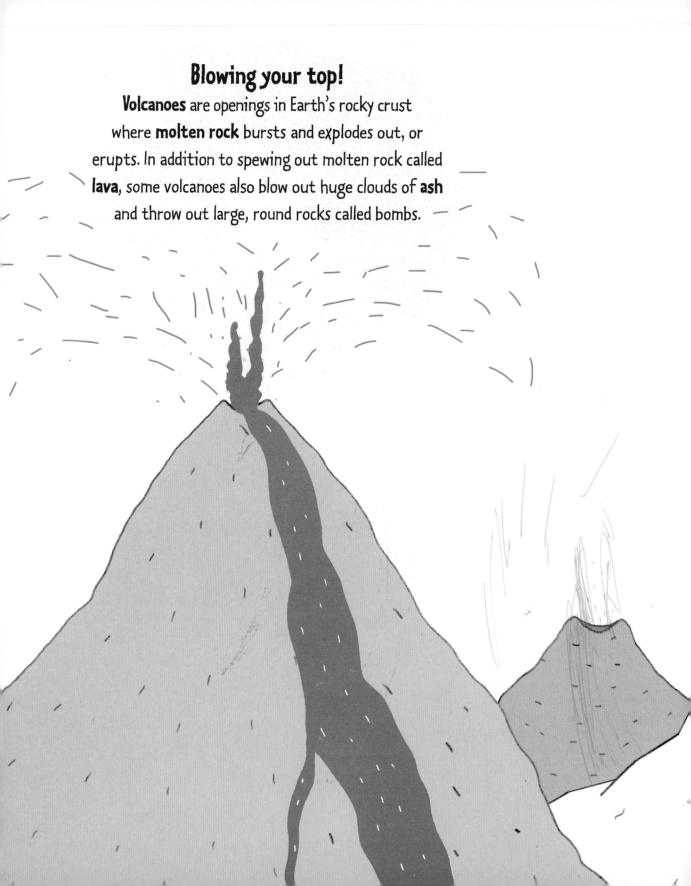

After an eruption, the released lava cools down and creates new rock, including:

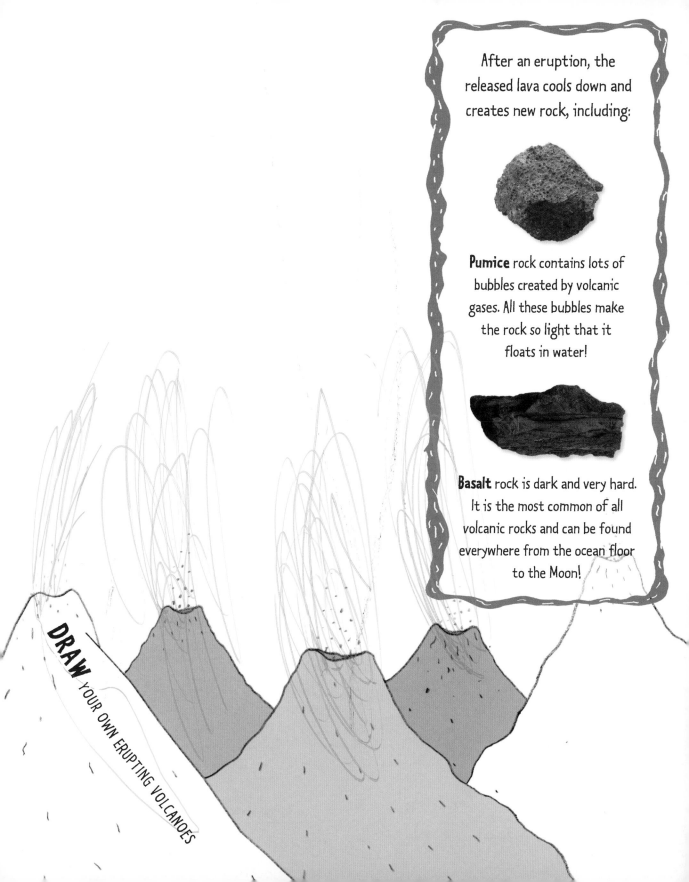

Pumice rock contains lots of bubbles created by volcanic gases. All these bubbles make the rock so light that it floats in water!

Basalt rock is dark and very hard. It is the most common of all volcanic rocks and can be found everywhere from the ocean floor to the Moon!

DRAW YOUR OWN ERUPTING VOLCANOES

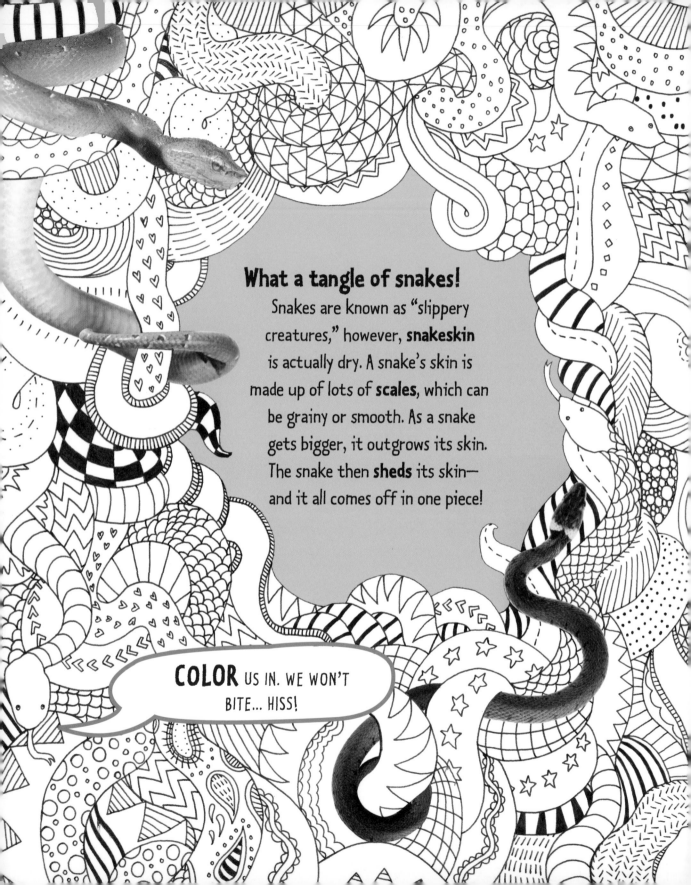

What a tangle of snakes!

Snakes are known as "slippery creatures," however, **snakeskin** is actually dry. A snake's skin is made up of lots of **scales**, which can be grainy or smooth. As a snake gets bigger, it outgrows its skin. The snake then **sheds** its skin— and it all comes off in one piece!

COLOR US IN. WE WON'T BITE... HISS!

Wall art!

In the beginning, early humans found a way to tell stories using art. But they didn't have paper so they used cave walls! Cave paintings have been found all over the world. The earliest cave paintings date from 33,000 BCE and were painted onto the walls of the Chauvet caves in France. The cave artists used their fingers, twigs, or leaves as brushes, and made paint from different colored soil, ash, and berries.

Some cave artists didn't use paints. Instead, they would **scratch away** the top **surface** of the cave to reveal a **lighter rock** underneath.

Men were drawn as **stick men**, but animals were more carefully drawn and colored in.

DRAW YOUR OWN STORIES ON THE CAVE WALL...

DESIGN YOUR OWN TOWN

The **most populated city** in the world is **Tokyo**, Japan. Just under 32.5 million people live there.

More than half of the world's population lives in towns and cities.

KEY

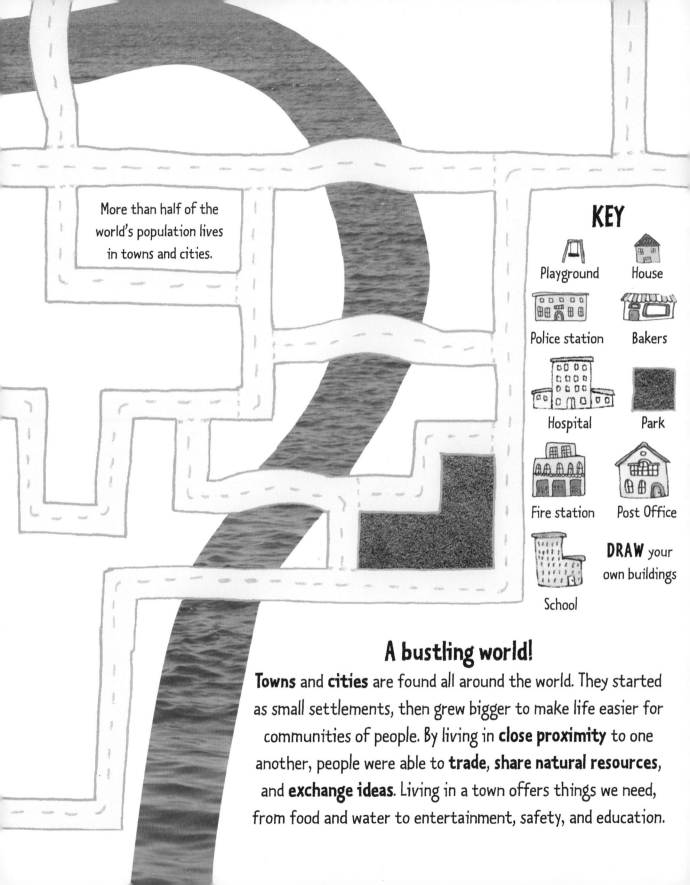

Playground

House

Police station

Bakers

Hospital

Park

Fire station

Post Office

School

DRAW your own buildings

A bustling world!

Towns and **cities** are found all around the world. They started as small settlements, then grew bigger to make life easier for communities of people. By living in **close proximity** to one another, people were able to **trade**, **share natural resources**, and **exchange ideas**. Living in a town offers things we need, from food and water to entertainment, safety, and education.

Many people claim to have spotted **UFOs** (unidentified flying objects) in the sky, but no claim has ever been proved to be true.

DRAW YOUR OWN SCI-FI MOVIE SCENE...

Science—fact or fiction?

Is there anybody out there? Scientists have long speculated about the existence of things like **aliens** and **time travel**. No one knows if these things are possible, so it's left to filmmakers to imagine what it would be like if they were. **Science fiction** movies (sci-fi) are based on science, often futuristic, and look at what would happen if aliens paid us a visit.

The symmetry of butterfly wings is known as **mirror symmetry**.

Butterfly wings are covered in tiny **scales**.

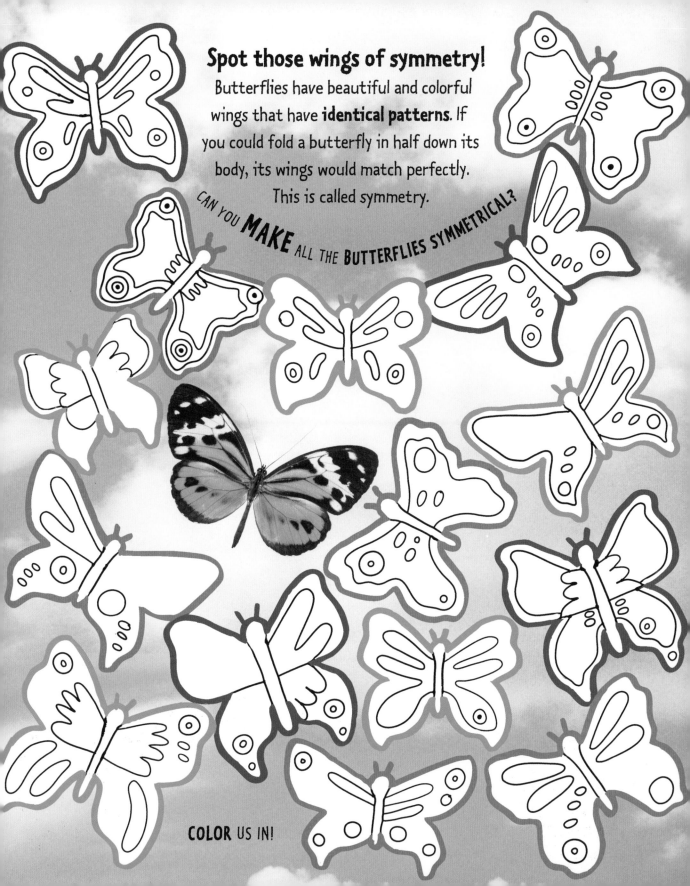

Spot those wings of symmetry!

Butterflies have beautiful and colorful wings that have **identical patterns**. If you could fold a butterfly in half down its body, its wings would match perfectly. This is called symmetry.

CAN YOU **MAKE** ALL THE **BUTTERFLIES SYMMETRICAL?**

COLOR US IN!

That sinking feeling!

Why might an apple **float**, but a pear **sink**? It all depends on the **weight** of the object and its **volume** (how much space it takes up). When an object is placed into water, the water has to move to make room for the object. This is called **displacement**. An object will **sink** because it's **heavier than the water** it has displaced. It will **float** if it weighs **less than the displaced water**.

A **cargo ship** is enormous, so why doesn't it sink? The ship's hull is **full of air**, so when the ship is launched into water, the **volume of water displaced is heavier than the ship**, so the ship floats.

The **physicist Archimedes** is believed to have discovered displacement when he sat in the bathtub, causing him to shout **"Eureka!"**

DRAW MORE THINGS THAT FLOAT OR SINK

SCRIBBLE CRAZY AND COOL **HAIRSTYLES** FOR THESE CHILLY-HEADED CHARACTERS...

... AND MAYBE SOME **MUSTACHES** AND **BEARDS**...

... HOW ABOUT DRAWING SOME **NASAL HAIR** (THAT'S THE HAIR IN YOUR NOSE)?...

... WHY NOT REALLY GO FOR IT AND **DOODLE** SOME **EAR HAIR?**

Hair-raising stuff! Hair is an amazing thing, and it's not just there to look good. Hair keeps you warm, protects parts of your body, and even keeps you clean. Hair will grow all over your body, except on your lips, palms of your hands, and soles of your feet.

A **man** has about **5,000,000** hair follicles (where hair attaches to the skin) all over **his body!**

DRAW ALL THE **JUNK** THAT IS **ORBITING** EARTH

An early piece of **rubbish** that floated in orbit was from the first American **space-walk**, when astronaut **Ed White** lost his **glove**!

No space for trash!
We are careful about throwing things away on Earth, but what about in space? At present, there is a jungle of **debris orbiting our planet**, from broken satellites to the remains of astronauts' lunch boxes. It's getting so crowded that the International Space Station has to dodge large chunks of space junk as it orbits Earth!

On safari!

Shhh! Keep very quiet! A **safari** is an overland journey usually across **Africa's grasslands**. It will bring you up close to the most amazing animals in the world. Africa is home to huge **herds** of **grazers**, such as **zebras**. They are hunted by **lions** and other **big cats**. **Scavengers**, such as **vultures**, clean up any leftovers.

A group of lions is called a **pride**. There can be up to 40 lions in one pride.

Many **safari animals** are in danger from **hunters**. Throughout Africa, **conservation movements** are in place to **protect** the animals.

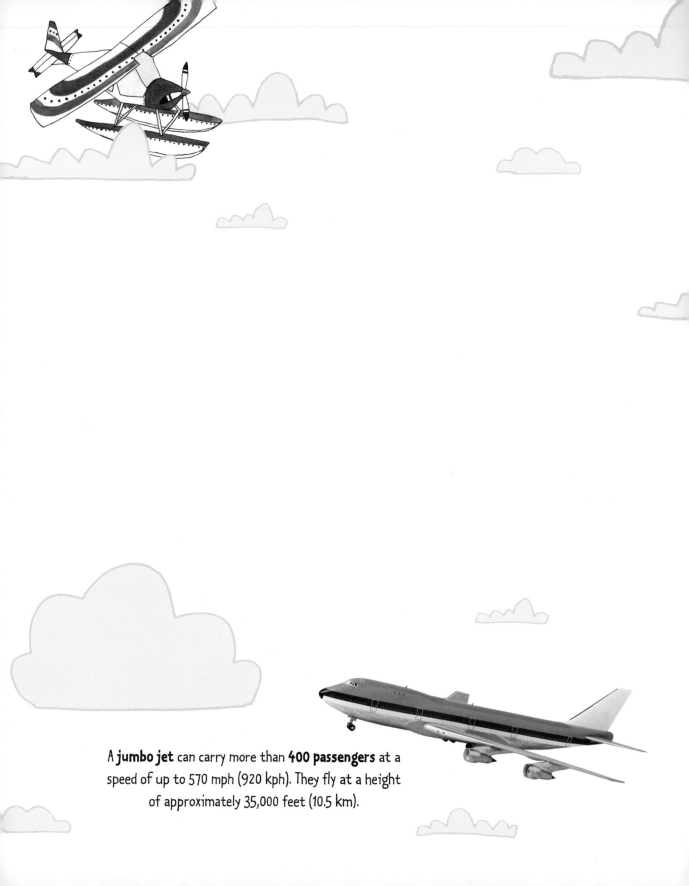

A **jumbo jet** can carry more than **400 passengers** at a speed of up to 570 mph (920 kph). They fly at a height of approximately 35,000 feet (10.5 km).

Is it a bird?

Airplanes are heavy, so how do they stay
in the sky? The engine and propeller create
a forward force call **thrust**. This moves air over
the wings, creating an upward force called **lift**.
Both **thrust and lift** must be **greater** than the opposing
forces of **drag and weight** for the airplane to fly.

LIFT

THRUST

DRAG

WEIGHT

DESIGN YOUR OWN
AIRCRAFT!

We are family

Arthropods make up 90 percent of all animal species in the world. There are four types of arthropod: **insects** (including dragonflies and beetles), **arachnids** (including spiders and scorpions), water-loving **crustaceans** (including crabs and lobsters), and **"-pedes"** (including centipedes and millipedes). Arthropods have **segmented bodies** (made up of more than one part) and are **cold-blooded** (they take on the temperature of their surroundings).

beetle

lobster

COLOR ALL THE INSECTS PURPLE

Green shield bugs are insects that can be found nibbling on plants.

dragonfly

COLOR ALL THE ARACHNIDS RED

spider

COLOR THE CRUSTACEANS BLUE

crab

scorpion

Some creepy crawlies have skeletons on the outside of their bodies. This skeleton is called an **exoskeleton**.

millipede

COLOR THE "-PEDES" YELLOW

centipede

HELP THE ARCHEOLOGIST FIND HIS WAY TO DISCOVER THE MUMMY

DRAW YOUR OWN EGYPTIAN TREASURE

Mummy method!

The **ancient Egyptians** believed in life after death, so they preserved the bodies of the dead through a process called **mummification**. Only Egyptian **pharaohs** (kings) and rich nobility could afford it. Turning a dead body into a "mummy" was a complicated and gruesome business. The body was washed and all the **organs were removed**, except the heart. It was then dried out using a salty mineral. Finally, it was wrapped in linen and placed in a decorative coffin called a **sarcophagus**—ready for the afterlife!

The organs removed from the body were stored in separate **canopic jars**, and buried with the mummy.

Mummified pharaohs were buried with all their valuable belongings, believing they would need them in the afterlife. To protect the mummy and its treasure from **tomb robbers**, elaborate mazes were built inside the tombs.

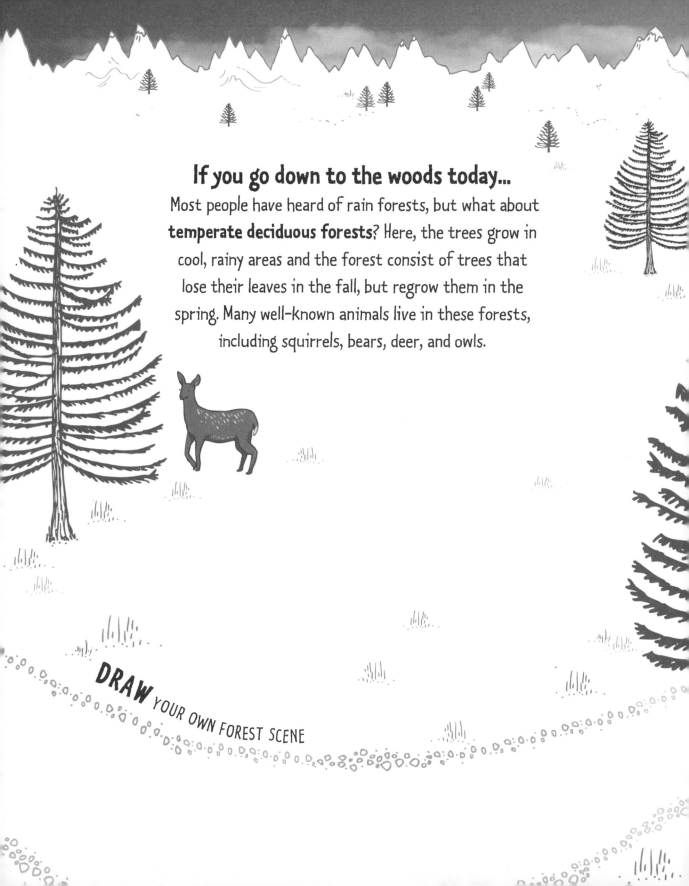

If you go down to the woods today...

Most people have heard of rain forests, but what about **temperate deciduous forests**? Here, the trees grow in cool, rainy areas and the forest consist of trees that lose their leaves in the fall, but regrow them in the spring. Many well-known animals live in these forests, including squirrels, bears, deer, and owls.

DRAW YOUR OWN FOREST SCENE

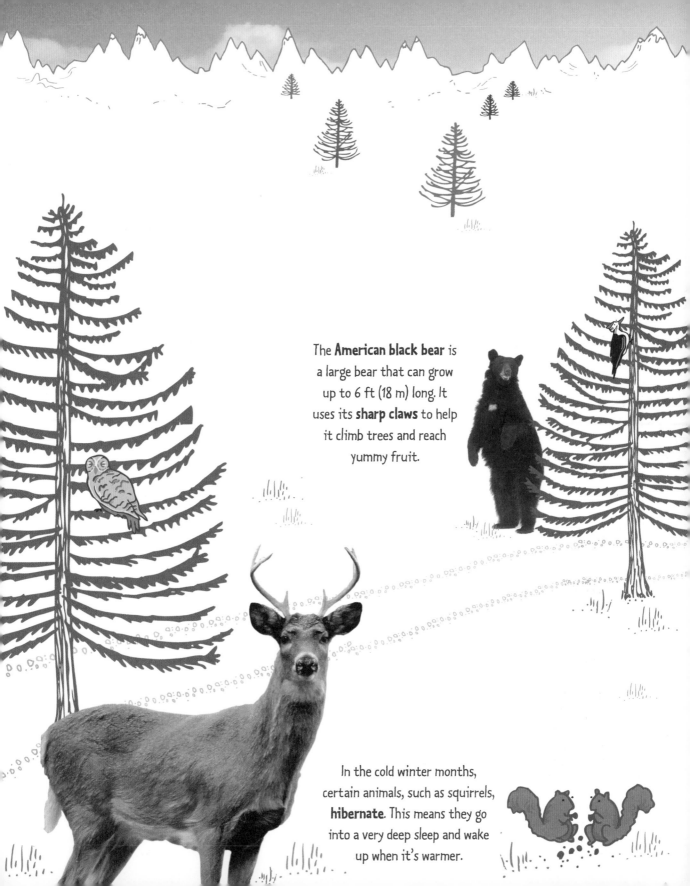

The **American black bear** is a large bear that can grow up to 6 ft (18 m) long. It uses its **sharp claws** to help it climb trees and reach yummy fruit.

In the cold winter months, certain animals, such as squirrels, **hibernate**. This means they go into a very deep sleep and wake up when it's warmer.

You, Robot!

Robots sound like something from a movie, but they are actually part of our lives today. Factories and businesses use robots to make things, doctors use them to **help in operations**, and scientists use them to **explore** places too dangerous for humans to go, such as Mars!

DESIGN YOUR OWN FUTURISTIC ROBOTS!

FINISH ME OFF!

Hi, I'm a hosting robot. You can hire me to host a party or event.

The bright colors produced by fireworks are created by the metallic chemicals inside them. **Copper** makes **blue** and **sodium** makes **yellow**.

Bang! Pop! Whizz!

Oooh! Ahh! **A firework** consists of **gunpowder** and different **metallic chemicals**, such as copper and sodium, wrapped up tightly in a paper tube with a **fuse**. Once the fuse is lit, the firework shoots high into the sky, and becomes hot, making all the chemicals **explode**, releasing their **energy** as **light**, **heat**, and **sound**.

DRAW AND **COLOR** YOUR OWN SPECTACULAR FIREWORKS DISPLAY

DRAW MORE BUSY BEES VISITING THE FLOWERS

FINISH AND **COLOR**
THE GARDEN

Bees are attracted to **bright, sweet-smelling** flowers. They drink the sugary **nectar** prodcued by the flower.

DON'T BUZZ OFF!

On a hot sunny day, buzzing bees can seem like a pain, especially if you get stung! But, in fact, bees are very important insects and vital for all plants. Bees are **pollinators and help plants reproduce.** When a bee lands on a flower to feed, the flower's **pollen** sticks to the bee's body, so when the bee lands on another flower, the pollen falls off and fertilizes the plant.

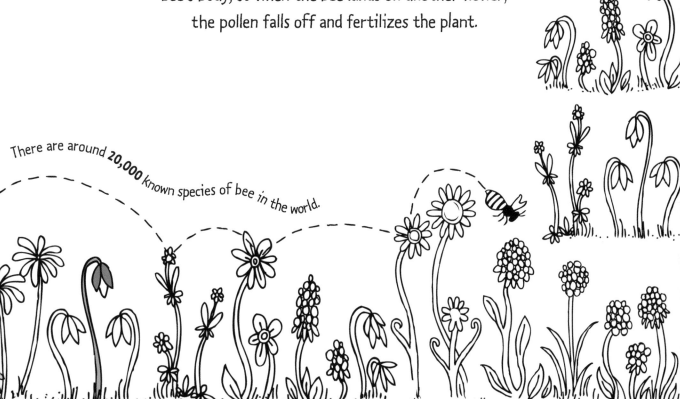

There are around **20,000** known species of bee in the world.

Flying high!

Birds make flying look so easy. How hard can it be? For centuries, humans tried to **fly like birds**. Early experiments included building "wings" made of **feathers** or **lightweight wood**. Attached to a brave volunteer, no matter how much the person flapped their arms, the wings didn't enable them to fly. Recent inventions include **jet packs** (or rocket packs), which lift the pilot off the ground vertically.

Astronauts on the International Space Station wear small jet packs called **"SAFERs."** The astronauts use the packs in an emergency, if they become detached from the station.

DRAW YOUR OWN FLYING MACHINE

COLOR THE SLAVES BLUE

FIND THE EMPEROR WATCHING HIS SUBJECTS AND WEARING HIS WREATH. **COLOR** HIM PURPLE

COLOR ALL THE GLADIATORS YELLOW

Romans rule!

Ancient Rome began as a group of small villages, and over several centuries grew into a **powerful empire**. Who was part of this mighty empire? It was ruled by an **emperor**, who made all the important decisions. The emperor was advised by the **consuls**, who were similar to today's **politicians**. Roman **gladiators** provided the nobility with **entertainment**, by fighting each other and wild animals to the death in huge arenas, such as the **Colosseum**. All the hard work was done by **slaves**, who were mostly prisoners captured by the Roman army.

COLOR ALL THE CONSULS RED

The Roman Empire created many things we still use today. **Roads**, **concrete**, and our **calendar** were all developed by the Romans.

Who's a pretty bird?

More than 1,500 species of bird live in the **Amazon rain forest**—that's one-third of all bird species in the world! This includes bright and vibrant birds such as **toucans** and **macaws**. The toucan's 8-in (19-cm) long colorful **beak** (bill) is useful for reaching and catching tasty fruit and bugs. Beautiful macaws are parrots and have powerful beaks that easily crack nuts and seeds.

Despite its impressive size, the toucan's beak is not very strong. It is made from a substance called **keratin** (the same substance that makes up human nails and hair) and is used to **intimidate** predators, rather than fight them.

COLOR THE RAIN FOREST BIRDS

DRAW SOMETHING
FANTASTIC
TO FINISH THE SECTION.

TURN THE PAGE FOR...

DOODLEPEDIA
DINOSAURS

DOODLEPEDIA
DINOSAURS

What is a dinosaur?

Long before humans existed, dinosaurs ruled the Earth. For millions of years, these amazing reptiles thrived. Dinosaurs came in all shapes and sizes, and there's still so much we don't know about them. In fact, it's very likely there are new and interesting species we have yet to discover. One thing is for certain though—they were all amazing!

DESIGN
YOUR OWN DINOSAURS.

Dinosaurs can be split into two categories: **ornithischians** (bird-hipped), and **saurischians** (lizard-hipped).

They all had **scaly skin,** but some of them also had **feathers.**

Most dinosaurs ate plants, but many were **meat-eaters**

Many dinosaurs were huge, but others were small.

Some walked on **two legs**, others walked on **four**.

All dinosaurs had **tails.**

All dinosaurs had **clawed or hooved** hands and feet.

The Mesozoic world

If you traveled back in time to see the rise of the dinosaurs, you'd need to go back about 250 million years to a period of the Earth's history called the **Mesozoic Era**. Back then, the Earth was **very different**, and all of the continents were joined together in one big supercontinent called **Pangaea**, which means "All Earth." The Mesozoic Era was divided into three periods: the Triassic, the Jurassic, and the Cretaceous. Each of these periods had its own climate and wildlife.

Because the Mesozoic era was so long, dinosaurs from different periods would have **never met**. In fact, more time separates Stegosaurus from T. rex, than T. rex from us!

DRAW A PICTURE OF YOURSELF IN THE TIME MACHINE.

Herrerasaurus

Coelophysis

Lesothosaurus

Mussaurus

TRIASSIC
(251–200 MILLION YEARS AGO).

Pterodactylus

Oviraptor

Velociraptor

HUMANS
65 MILLION YEARS IN THE FUTURE.

Brachiosaurus

COLOR
ALL THE DINOSAURS.

Pachycephalosaurus

Tyrannosaurus rex
(T. rex)

Triceratops

Stegosaurus

Spinosaurus

Eoraptor

Iguanodon

CRETACEOUS
(145–65 MILLION YEARS AGO).

JURASSIC (200–145 MILLION YEARS AGO).

The Earth was very **dry** during the Triassic period. Only the coasts and valleys saw much water.

FINISH THE REST OF THE TRIASSIC SCENE.

Herrerasaurus

Eoraptor

GRRR

We don't have any photos to show us what life was like back then. Everything we know we learn from **studying the remains** of prehistoric things (fossils).

Plateosaurus

The Triassic period

The Earth's scenery was very different during the **Triassic period** (between 251–200 million years ago). It was very hot and the land was covered in large patches of desert, with no grass or flowers and only a few plants. It was during the early Triassic period that the first dinosaurs, such as the Eoraptor **(EE-oh-rap-tor)**, Plateosaurus **(PLATE-ee-oh-SORE-us)**, and Herrerasaurus **(her-RARE-uh-SORE-us)** first emerged.

The Jurassic period

By the time the Triassic period ended 200 million years ago, the Earth had **changed dramatically**. The supercontinent Pangaea **split apart**, creating new continents, oceans, and seas. This made the planet's temperature cool, causing **deserts to shrink and lush forests to grow**. These changes created a lot more food for wildlife. As a result, the Jurassic period saw many **new species** of dinosaur appear.

COLOR IN THE DINOSAURS.

It was during the Jurassic period that the stout Stegosaurus (STEG-oh-SORE-uss), the fierce Allosaurus (al-oh-SORE-us), and the supersized Brachiosaurus (brackee-oh-SORE-uss) existed.

The Cretaceous period

The longest period of the Mesozoic Era was the Cretaceous, which spanned from 145–65 million years ago. It was a time of **incredible diversity**, when many new species of dinosaur appeared. One reason for this was that the continents that formed when Pangaea split drifted farther apart, **spreading dinosaurs to new corners of the Earth.** At the time, the continents were still different from the way they are today, but they were starting to look more like they do now.

PRESENT DAY

North America · Europe · Asia · Africa · South America · Australia · Antarctica

COLOR
THE CONTINENTS AND TRY TO MATCH EACH MODERN VERSION.

Triceratops

DRAW MORE DINOSAURS ON THE MAP.

The Cretaceous period was when some of the most well-known dinosaurs lived, including Tyrannosaurus rex, Triceratops, and Velociraptor.

The Earth's continents are still moving today, just very slowly!

Tyrannosaurus rex

Herbivores

The word dinosaur means "terrible lizard," but that doesn't mean they were all terrible! It's true that many dinosaurs were predators, but most were actually **plant-eaters** (herbivores). By the time the Jurassic period rolled around, the Earth was covered with forests—or to a herbivore, **free dinner** for the taking! They just had to get there before all the other dinosaurs showed up!

The biggest dinosaurs of all, sauropods ate only plants. They had to graze **all day** to get enough fuel. It's amazing there was enough food to go around!

DRAW MORE DINOSAURS GETTING THEIR DINNER.

CYCADS

BABY GINGKOS

FERNS

DRAW FOOD IN THE DINOSAURS' GROCERY CARTS BEFORE IT'S ALL GONE!

Carnivores

While the majority of dinosaurs happily munched on plants, carnivores (meat-eaters) survived by eating lizards, insects, and other dinosaurs. Although many carnivores had similar dining habits, this was not always the case. For example, Compsognathus **(COMP-sog-NAITH-us)**, was about the size of a chicken and scavenged a lot of its meals, but the monstrous Carnotaurus **(CAR-no-TORE-us)** was nearly twice as big as a man. Imagine how much it would need to eat to get full!

DRAW A MEAL FOR THE HUNGRY CARNOTAURUS.

Smaller carnivores sometimes had to **scavenge** for their meat.

Carnivores had large hearts and lungs that helped them take in lots of oxygen. This made it easier for them to hunt! Remember, their dinner could run away from them!

SAVE THE TENONTOSAURUS.
DRAW A SAFE ROUTE OUT OF THE FOREST.

START

Pack attack

Not all predators were big. Sometimes they were **smaller than their prey**! (Imagine your dinner being bigger than you!) To turn the tables, dinosaurs such as Deinonychus **(dye-NON-ee-cuss)** would hunt together, finding prey that had been separated from its **herd** and ganging up on it before moving in for the kill.

FINISH

Deinonychus and Velociraptor were among the deadliest pack hunters.

COLOR

THE FOREST AND CAMOUFLAGE THE SCUTELLOSAURUS.

Habitats

The world of the dinosaurs was very different from ours. Dinosaurs lived in all kinds of **environments** and were always looking for the right place to call **home**.

COLOR THE DESERT.

Deserts—the Earth's climate was **warmer** than it is today, and large areas of desert were found throughout the Mesozoic era.

DRAW MORE DINOSAURS OCCUPYING THE SCRUBLAND.

Scrubland—This **semidesert** supported plants that didn't require much water to survive and was home for many early species of dinosaur.

Too steep!

FINISH THE REST OF THE MOUNTAIN RANGE.

Mountains—These appeared at a growing rate as the Earth's **plates shifted** over the years, but it's likely there wasn't a great deal of food there.

COLOR THE CROC.

Swampland—Swamps were very common throughout the Cretaceous period and were home to **hadrosaurs** and many other herbivores.

Too wet!

FINISH THE RIVER.

Riverbanks—All living things need water to survive, so a lot of dinosaurs settled close to **riverbanks** and **coasts**.

Perfect! Home, sweet home!

FINISH THE FOREST AND **DRAW** ANOTHER TRICERATOPS.

Forests—Even though dense forests would have helped predators to blend in, they were a **rich source of food** for herbivores such as Triceratops **(try-SERRA-tops).**

Therizinosaurus

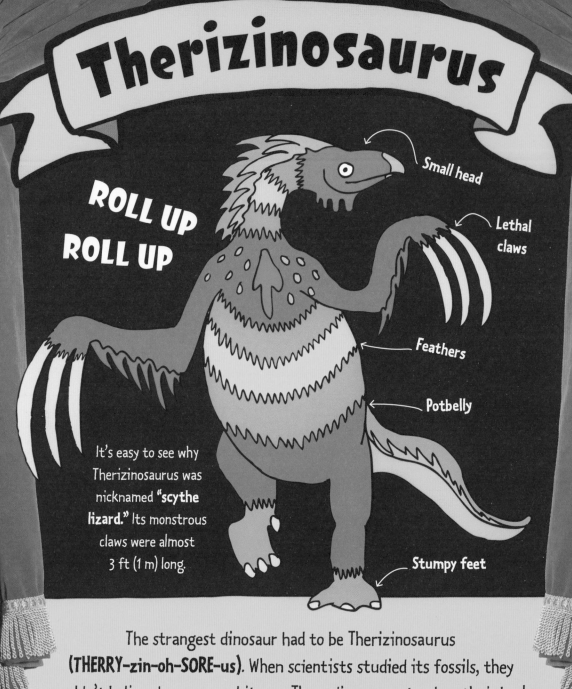

**ROLL UP
ROLL UP**

Small head

Lethal claws

Feathers

Potbelly

It's easy to see why Therizinosaurus was nicknamed **"scythe lizard."** Its monstrous claws were almost 3 ft (1 m) long.

Stumpy feet

The strangest dinosaur had to be Therizinosaurus **(THERRY-zin-oh-SORE-us)**. When scientists studied its fossils, they couldn't believe how unusual it was. These dinosaurs stood on their back legs like most predators, but only ate plants. They had lethal claws, but didn't use them for hunting. They had small heads, feathers, stumpy feet, and their large digestive systems gave them big **potbellies!** How weird!

DRAW AND NAME AN EVEN WEIRDER DINOSAUR OF YOUR OWN!

Crests and plumes

Many dinosaurs had impressive crests and plumes on their heads to **attract mates** and to **threaten rivals**. They came in all shapes and sizes. Can you picture how they might have looked?

PARASAUROLOPHUS

Guanlong **(GWON-long),** an early relative of Tyrannosaurus rex, was discovered in China in 2006.

GUANLONG

CRYOLOPHOSAURUS

DRAW CRESTS AND PLUMES ON THE DINOSAURS, THEN MAKE UP YOUR OWN AND GIVE THEM NAMES.

Sticking together

For herbivores, danger lurked around every corner. Plant-eaters such as Tenontosaurus **(ten-NON-toe-SORE-us)** that weren't able to defend themselves looked for **safety in numbers**. They traveled in herds to make sneaky predators think twice about attacking them.

Modern animals such as zebras and wildebeests travel in herds for the same reason.

FINISH THE REST OF THE TENONTOSAURUS HERD.

Bone dome

Pachycephalosaurus **(PACK-ee-sef-ah-low-SORE-us)** was famous for a very unusual feature. They had a huge, thick skull shaped a little like a **bowling ball**, which might look ugly, but don't tell them that! Experts believe this strange dome was used like a **battering ram** to discourage predators and to intimidate rivals, similar to how stags butt heads today. It's also possible, however, that it was just for show.

The dome was made of **solid bone** and was 10 in (25 cm) thick!

The word pachycephalosaur means "thick-headed lizard."

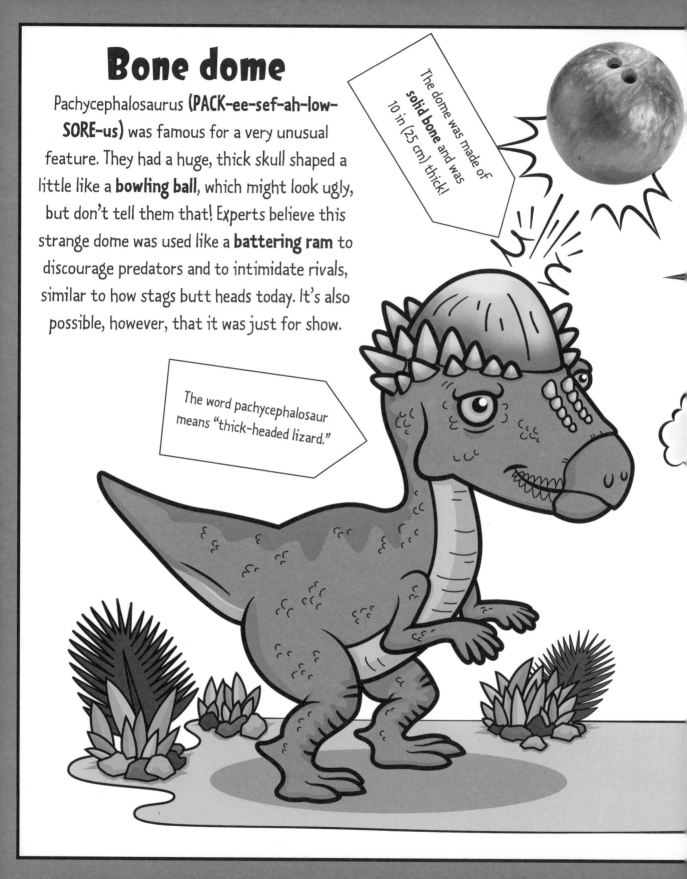

DRAW ANOTHER YOUNG PACHYCEPHALOSAURUS PLAY FIGHTING.

Walking weapons

Danger was everywhere during the time of the dinosaurs—even predators were sometimes **prey for bigger dinosaurs themselves!** Only the biggest and strongest such as Tyrannosaurus rex could feel safe at all times. The scariest predators didn't need any special weapons to take down their prey—they had their own!

T. rex's jaw was so powerful that it could **crush the bones** of its prey with ease.

Allosaurus had a weak jaw, but very sharp teeth. It's possible it **slashed** its prey rather than try to bite it.

Many types of **raptor** had claws so sharp that their prey wouldn't have stood a chance against them.

DRAW YOUR OWN DINOSAURS WITH DEADLY WEAPONS.

Defense

No dinosaur wanted to be an easy meal. Some would try to fight off predators with their claws and teeth, but others—such as a group of dinosaur called **ankylosaurs**—had special defensive features such as plates and spines. One of these was Euoplocephalus **(YOU-owe-plo-SEFF-ah-luss)**, which was **built like a tank** and had a crushing club made of bone at the end of its tail that it would swing at attacking predators.

Euoplocephalus was so armored with spikes and plates that even its **eyelids** were protected!

DESIGN YOUR OWN ARMORED DINOSAUR.

FIGHTING BACK

When under attack from predators, dinosaurs were faced with a choice: to either **run or fight.** And sometimes the best defense was a good offense. Several herbivores had more than just armor and were equipped with deadly weapons of their own to help them **fight back** against their enemies.

STEGOSAURUS

Stegosaurus had **razor-sharp** spikes on its tail, which it could whip at enemies.

PENTACERATOPS

Pentaceratops and other ceratopsians could use their large **horns** as weapons of defense.

IGUANODON

Iguanodon had sharp **spikes** on its hands to jab at attackers.

DIPLODOCUS

Not only was Diplodocus huge, but it could also use its long tail like a **whip**.

DRAW THE FIGHTING DINOSAURS.

FINISH
DRAWING THE
SPINES ON
THE DINOSAURS.

OURANOSAURUS

Spines and sails

It wasn't just their teeth and claws that helped dinosaurs stand out. Several dinosaurs had sail-like spines on their backs and necks. While these would have mainly been used to **attract mates** and **scare off rivals**, experts believe that they might also have helped dinosaurs manage their body temperature.

RAYOSOSAURUS

SPINOSAURUS

One of the most impressive spines belonged to **Spinosaurus,** the largest predator ever to walk the Earth. It was **even bigger** than Tyrannosaurus rex!

Mini monster

Who says you had to be big to be a predator? Compsognathus **(COMP-sog-NAITH-us)**, a predator from the Jurassic period, was no bigger than a **chicken**! It used its speed and agility to chase down fast-moving lizards and insects, scavenge other predators' kills, and even sometimes **gang up on** and take down larger prey.

It may have been small, but it was fast. Despite its size, Compsognathus could **run at speeds of more than 25 mph** (40 kph).

25

DRAW

THE REST OF THE
COMPSOGNATHUS PACK.

Compsognathus may have
been covered in **feathers,
fuzz,** or **scales** to help
it stay warm.

Grazing giants

The Jurassic period saw the rise of the sauropods—the largest creatures ever to walk the Earth. The largest of these, Argentinosaurus (ARE-jen-teen-oh-SORE-us), grew to 120 ft (36 m) long and weighed as much as **13 elephants**. It would have needed to eat all day to have enough energy to move!

A single Brachiosaurus would have had to eat around 400 lb (180 kg) of food **every day!**

COLOR
ARGENTINOSAURUS GREEN.

COLOR
DIPLODOCUS RED.

Sauropods had long necks so they could reach food other dinosaurs couldn't. Some could even stand on their **hind legs**!

Sauropods were plant-eaters, but that doesn't mean they couldn't defend themselves from predators. They were so massive that they could **crush** any attackers.

COLOR
BRACHIOSAURUS YELLOW.

COLOR
SALTASAURUS BLUE.

Titans of the Earth

Tyrannosaurus rex gets all the glory, but plenty of other giant predators existed. In fact, T. rex's "cousin" Giganotosaurus (**gig-AN-oh-toe-SORE-rus**) was just as big. It's lucky they lived 10 million years apart or there would have been **nasty fights** at mealtimes!

Experts believe that Giganotosaurus had a brain the shape of a **banana!**

No complete Giganotosaurus skeleton has been found, but experts believe these giants were about 45 ft (13.5 m) long and weighed as much as **125 people!**

COLOR CARNOTAURUS RED.

COLOR GIGANOTOSAURUS BLUE.

COLOR TYRANNOSAURUS GREEN.

COLOR TYRANNOTITAN YELLOW.

COLOR CARCHARODONTOSAURUS PURPLE.

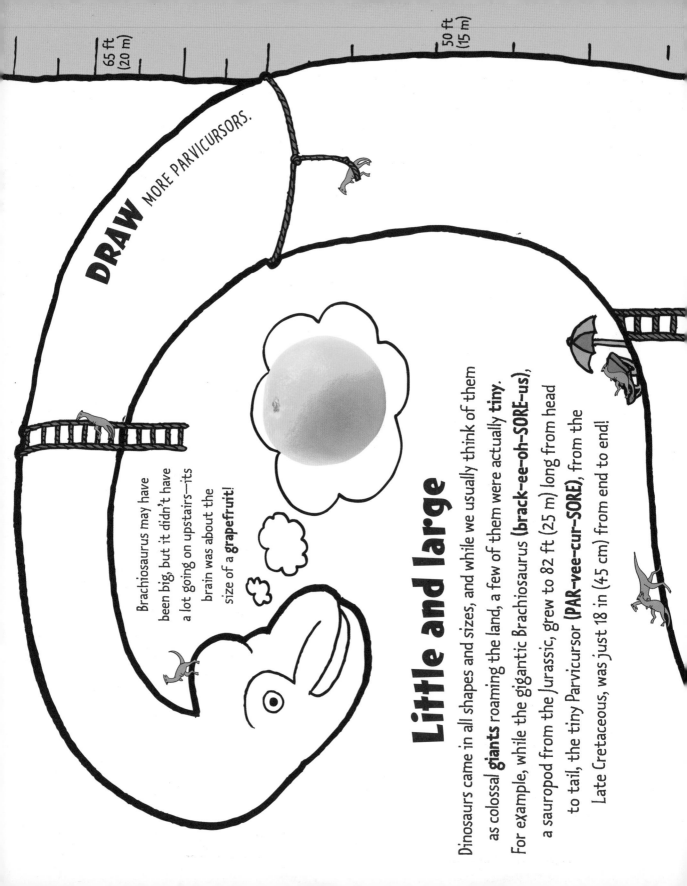

DRAW MORE PARVICURSORS.

Brachiosaurus may have been big, but it didn't have a lot going on upstairs—its brain was about the size of a **grapefruit!**

Little and large

Dinosaurs came in all shapes and sizes, and while we usually think of them as colossal **giants** roaming the land, a few of them were actually **tiny.**

For example, while the gigantic Brachiosaurus (**brack–ee–oh–SORE–us**), a sauropod from the Jurassic, grew to 82 ft (25 m) long from head to tail, the tiny Parvicursor (**PAR–vee–cur–SORE**), from the Late Cretaceous, was just 18 in (45 cm) from end to end!

Parvicursors had fairly large claws on their hands, but these were probably used for **digging** rather than for defense.

Fast and slow

Fossils give us clues about how fast dinosaurs could run. Speed varied between species, and while no dinosaur could sprint like the fastest modern land animal, the **cheetah**, which can run at **70 mph** (114 kph), smaller dinosaurs were probably very fast. Others, such as the giant sauropods, were slow pokes.

Brachiosaurus weighed so much that it likely couldn't move faster than 3.5 mph (6 kph)!

Brachiosaurus

Ankylosaurus was built like a tank and **didn't need to** run away from predators, so it was probably slow-moving.

Ankylosaurus

DRAW MORE RACING DINOSAURS.

Predators walked on two legs to be able to move fast enough to catch their food.

Predator and prey

All dinosaurs had to eat to survive, and while herbivores were happy to chomp on plants, carnivores had something a little fresher in mind! Because of this, plant-eaters were always on the lookout for **hungry predators** ready to turn them into their next meal!

CAN YOU TELL THE HUNTERS FROM THE HUNTED?
COLOR THE PREDATORS ORANGE AND THE PREY YELLOW.

Herbivores were slow-moving and walked on four legs.

Stegosaurus

Don't let the fact that Stegosaurus **(STEG-oh-SORE-uss)** was a plant-eater trick you into thinking it was easy prey. Stegosauruses grew to 30 ft (9 m) long and weighed as much as **4.5 tons.** (4 metric tons). With their impressive plates and **sharp, spiked tails**, they were well-equipped to fend off even the fiercest predators of the Jurassic period.

FINISH THE SPIKES ON THE TAIL.

HELP THE STEGOSAURUS FIGHT OFF THE ALLOSAURUS.
DRAW MORE DEFENSIVE PLATES.

Stegosaurus certainly wasn't the smartest dinosaur in the herd. Its brain was no bigger than a **walnut!**

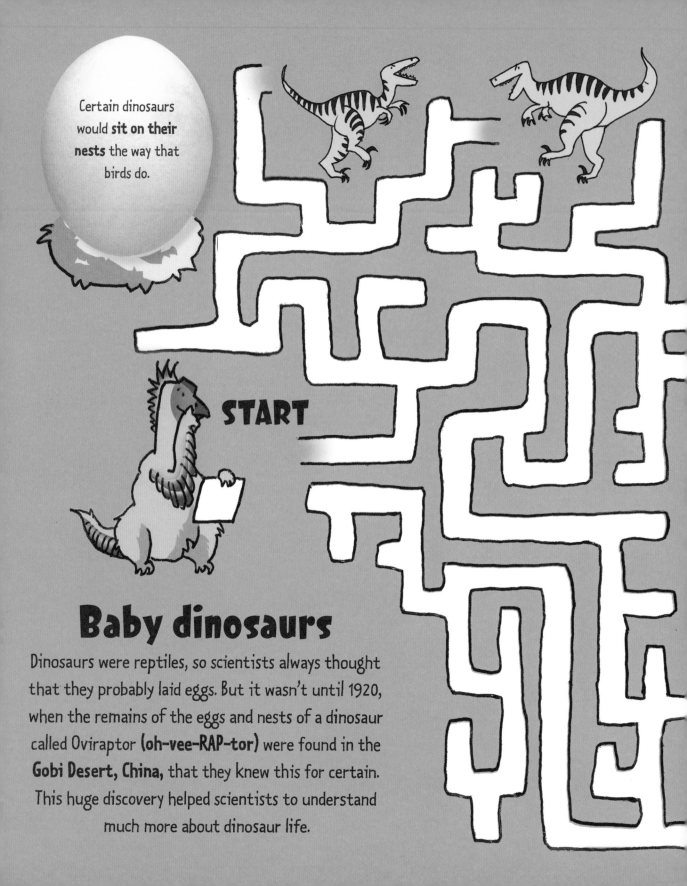

Certain dinosaurs would **sit on their nests** the way that birds do.

START

Baby dinosaurs

Dinosaurs were reptiles, so scientists always thought that they probably laid eggs. But it wasn't until 1920, when the remains of the eggs and nests of a dinosaur called Oviraptor **(oh-vee-RAP-tor)** were found in the **Gobi Desert, China,** that they knew this for certain. This huge discovery helped scientists to understand much more about dinosaur life.

The temperature of dinosaur eggs helped **determine the gender** of the babies. The warmer the eggs, the more likely it was that they would hatch as males.

DRAW THE OVIRAPTOR A SAFE ROUTE BACK TO HER NEST.

FINISH

Oviraptor would sometimes dig its nests in sand or soil.

Parasaurolophus

During the Cretaceous period, a group of dinosaur called hadrosaurs, or "duck-billed" dinosaurs, emerged. Among these was Parasaurolophus **(PA-ra-SORE-oh-LOAF-uss)**, a large plant-eater with hundreds of grinding teeth for mashing up food. They were common and traveled in large herds and are sometimes thought of as the dinosaur version of cows!

Unlike most other herbivores, hadrosaurs could walk on either two or four legs.

Parasaurolophus was **surprisingly big** for prey, and adults could grow to be 33 ft (10 m) long. No wonder it was a favorite meal for many carnivores—it made for very big portions!

CONNECT THE DOTS TO REVEAL THE PICTURE.

No one is certain if dinosaurs **communicated with sound**, but experts believe they probably did. One reason for this is that Parasaurolophus's crest contained a series of tubes that **connected to the nostrils**—which meant it might have worked like a trumpet.

Deinonychus

While teeth were the weapon of choice for many dinosaurs, others inflicted damage with their **claws**. Perhaps the scariest of these dinosaurs was Deinonychus **(dye-NON-ee-cuss)**, a speedy pack hunter from the Early Cretaceous. In addition to the sharp claws on its hands, Deinonychus had a monstrous upturned **sickle claw** on each foot that it used to deliver lethal strikes.

Deinonychus means "terrible claw," and it's easy to see why!

Deinonychus was a fierce hunter, but it was only 10 ft (3 m) long, so it roamed in packs to take down larger prey.

FINISH THE REST OF THE DEINONYCHUS PACK.

The long tail was held stiff to help with balance while running.

Dressed to frill

Known for their **horns** and neck frills, ceratopsians were a group of herbivores from the Cretaceous period. They might look scary, but their large frills and horns were **only for protection**, and their sharp beaks were used to **rip up plants** for food.

Although they look a little similar, ceratopsians are not related to the modern **rhinoceros**.

COLOR
PROTOCERATOPS GREEN.

There is lots of fossil evidence to suggest that many **fierce battles** took place between Triceratops and T. rex.

COLOR
STYRACOSAURUS PURPLE.

COLOR
PENTACERATOPS BLUE.

Pentaceratops had a **giant skull** measuring 10 ft (3 m) long!

COLOR TRICERATOPS RED.

COLOR CHASMOSAURUS YELLOW.

The ultimate predator

Tyrannosaurus rex **(TIE-ran-oh-SORE-us)**, or T. rex for short, was a ferocious hunter with a massive skull and **bone-crushing teeth**. At 13 ft (4 m) tall and 40 ft (12 m) long, it weighed as much as **five cars**. It was one of the biggest predators that ever lived, and it terrorized the forests of what is now North America until it became extinct 65 million years ago. Phew!

FINISH THE T. REX'S DINNER INSIDE ITS STOMACH.

Pterosaurs

Pterosaurs (**teh-ROH-sores**) weren't dinosaurs; they were flying creatures that ruled the skies in the age of the dinosaurs. They were the first **vertebrates** (animals with backbones) to fly. Ranging in size from sparrows to airplanes, the biggest pterosaurs were the biggest animals ever known to fly. They **terrorized** the skies, swooping over the sea, scooping up fish and other sea creatures, or scavenging for food on land.

COLOR
SORDES
GREEN.

COLOR
PTERODACTYLUS
PURPLE.

COLOR

TUPANDACTYLUS YELLOW.

COLOR

GERMANODACTYLUS BLUE.

COLOR

DORYGNATHUS RED.

Quetzalcoatlus was a **soarer** rather than a flier. It relied on strong winds to travel through the air.

DRAW MORE SOARING QUETZALCOATLUSES.

Quetzalcoatlus

The largest creature ever to fly was the monstrous pterosaur Quetzalcoatlus **(KWETS-ul-coe-AT-luss)**. This giant ruled the Cretaceous skies, casting a wide shadow over the ground wherever it flew. Its **wingspan** was a massive 40 ft (12 m) across, the size of a small plane!

The first bird

Believe it or not, birds are the descendants of dinosaurs. Technically, **they are dinosaurs**—the only surviving group! The earliest known bird is Archaeopteryx **(ar-kee-OP-ter-ix)**, which appeared in the Jurassic period. It had the feathered tail and wings of a bird, but the claws of a dinosaur.

COLOR
IN THE FUNKY FEATHERS.

Archaeopteryx was about the same size as a modern raven.

No one knows what color their feathers were. For all we know they could have been **bright pink or orange!**

COLOR
TYLOSAURUS PURPLE.

COLOR
PLESIOSAURUS BLUE.

Creatures of the deep

Dinosaurs ruled the land, and pterosaurs dominated the sky, but it was **marine reptiles** that **lurked beneath the waves** during the Mesozoic Era. The largest of these massive monsters could grow to 65 ft (20 m) long, and although they spent their lives in the water, they all **breathed air.**

The skull of Deinosuchus (**die-no-SUE-kus**)—a relative of modern crocodiles—was 6 ft (1.8 m) long, and a full-grown Deinosuchus weighed up to 5.5 tons (5 metric tons)!

COLOR DEINOSUCHUS YELLOW.

COLOR ELASMOSAURUS RED.

Elasmosaurus had **72 bones** in its neck!

COLOR KRONOSAURUS GREEN.

Rhomaleosaurus

The words "sea monsters" come to mind when you think of Rhomaleosaurus **(ROME-alley-oh-SORE-us).** They grew to up to 21 ft (7 m) long and in many ways were like the aquatic version of Tyrannosaurus rex. They **terrorized** the Jurassic seas, feasting on fish, squid, and smaller marine reptiles.

Rhomaleosaurus glided through the water using its four flippers like wings to **"fly"** underwater. Penguins and sea lions do a similar thing today.

CONNECT THE DOTS TO REVEAL THE PICTURE.

It's thought that like a lot of ocean predators, Rhomaleosaurus had a pale belly and dark back, making it **harder to spot** from both above and below.

Megatooth

If you thought plesiosaurs were scary, you're in for a shock. Megatooth **(MEG-a-tooth)**, an ancestor of the great white shark, may have existed 40 million years after the time of the dinosaurs, pterosaurs, and marine reptiles, but it was the all-time **ultimate monster of the deep**. It grew to 65 ft (20 m) long, weighed up to 110 tons (100 metric tons), and is probably the most ferocious predator ever.

START

Megatooth's teeth were the size of dinner plates, and it had about **250** of them. That would mean a lot of toothpaste!

FINISH

DRAW A WAY OUT OF THE MEGATOOTH MAZE.

Great white shark

The ultimate beast!

All dinosaurs were amazing creatures, but some dinosaurs were a little more spectacular than others. These dinosaurs were among the **fastest, strongest, scariest, and most interesting** to have lived—but can you imagine what a dinosaur with all of these qualities combined would be like?

LONGEST NECK
MAMENCHISAURUS

PERIOD	JURASSIC
SIZE	★★★★★
SPEED	★
INTELLIGENCE	★★

BIGGEST BRAIN
TROODON

PERIOD	CRETACEOUS
SIZE	★
SPEED	★★★★
INTELLIGENCE	★★★★★

STRONGEST BITE
T. REX

PERIOD	CRETACEOUS
SIZE	★★★★
SPEED	★★★
INTELLIGENCE	★

DRAW THE SCARIEST DINOSAURS THAT NEVER LIVED BY COMBINING THE FEATURES OF THE OTHER DINOSAURS.

BEST ARMOR
ANKYLOSAURUS

PERIOD	CRETACEOUS
SIZE	★★★
SPEED	★★
INTELLIGENCE	★★

DEADLIEST CLAWS
UTAHRAPTOR

PERIOD	CRETACEOUS
SIZE	★★★
SPEED	★★★★
INTELLIGENCE	★★★

FASTEST LEGS
STRUTHIOMIMUS

PERIOD	CRETACEOUS
SIZE	★★
SPEED	★★★★★
INTELLIGENCE	★★★★

Where did they go?

At the end of the Cretaceous period, dinosaurs were **thriving** like never before. Then, about 65 million years ago—with the exception of several species of bird—they **mysteriously died out**. The reason why this happened puzzled scientists for years, but they now believe that a **massive meteorite** crashed into the Earth. This caused earthquakes, tsunamis, volcanic eruptions, and threw up a cloud of dust so big that it blocked out the Sun.

The **remains of a crater** 112 miles (180 km) wide can be found in Mexico. Experts believe this is where the meteorite crash-landed.

EEEK

DRAW MORE SCARED DINOSAURS!

Other theories about why the dinosaurs became extinct include an ice age and a dinosaur **plague**.

Scientists estimate that the meteorite would have been roughly 6 miles (10 km) wide and struck the Earth at a **staggering** 60,000 mph (100,000 kph)!

THE DAILY DINO

WHAT SURVIVED?

SEE THE LATEST IN DINOSAUR FASHION!

In the millions of years that followed the destruction of the dinosaurs, many new species of animal **came and went**. However, a handful of creatures, other than birds from the Mesozoic Era, managed to **survive the extinction** and are still around today—on land, in the sea, and in the air.

DRAW THE REST OF THE SURVIVORS.

Various species of **fish, shark, and jellyfish** were among the creatures that survived in the seas.

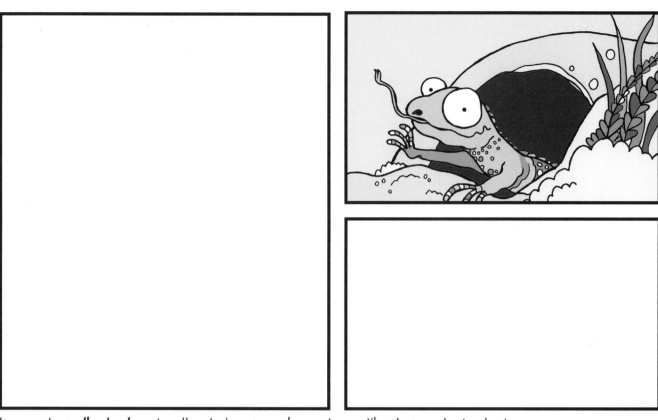

It was only **small animals** such as lizards, insects, snakes, and crocodiles that survived on land.

While a lot of **early birds** became extinct, a few species managed to survive, and so did many flying insects.

FINISH

A MODERN CITY WITH PEOPLE AND DINOSAURS LIVING TOGETHER!

What if they weren't extinct?

In the years that followed the extinction caused by the meteorite, the world became a **very different** place. The continents shifted, the climate changed, and thousands of new species of animal and plant evolved. Eventually, human beings emerged and became the Earth's most **dominant species.** But can you imagine what the world would be like if the dinosaurs hadn't become extinct? Would we keep dinosaurs as pets? Or would they be destructive and try to eat us?

Turning to stone

Everything we know about dinosaurs, pterosaurs, and marine reptiles we learned from their **fossilized remains**. Fossils are the stone remnants of things that lived long ago and that have been preserved in the Earth's layers.

Tyrannosaurus rex (T. rex)

Velociraptor

Brachiosaurus

Edaphosaurus

People who study fossils are called **paleontologists.**

Fossils are rare. Most dinosaurs simply decayed and **disappeared forever**. Only a few of the dinosaurs that lived have been, or will be found, as fossils.

Triceratops

Pterodactylus

DRAW MORE FOSSILS IN THE EARTH.

Fossilized eggs, feathers, footprints, and even **dinosaur poop** have been found. These all help us to understand more about prehistoric life.

Studying fossils

Not only are fossils **rare**, but they're also very fragile, and it takes a lot of hard work and patience for **paleontologists** (fossil experts) to get them out of the ground. When a fossil is discovered, huge dig sites are set up, and it can take months before the fossils are fully excavated for study in a lab.

Fossils are usually encased in rock, so paleontologists need a lot of tools to dig them out without breaking them.

FINISH THE OTHER HALF OF THE BURIED FOSSIL.

Dinosaurs on display

The dinosaurs might not be around anymore, but that shouldn't stop you from seeing what they were like. Museums have incredible dinosaur exhibits on display, including fossils that are **hundreds of millions** of years old, and even full skeletons!

SOME OF THE T. REX BONES HAVE FALLEN OFF! **DRAW** THEM BACK ON TO FINISH THE DISPLAY.

"Sue" the T. rex fossil at the Field Museum, Chicago, is the most complete T. rex fossil in the world. It cost the museum a whopping **$8.4 million** when they bought it in 1997.

TYRANNOSAURUS REX

Draw your own dinosaur

Now that you've learned all about these amazing creatures, draw **one of your own**. Who knows, one day a paleontologist might discover one that looks just like it!

DESIGN, COLOR, AND NAME YOUR OWN DINOSAUR.

DRAW SOMETHING
FANTASTIC
TO FINISH THE SECTION.

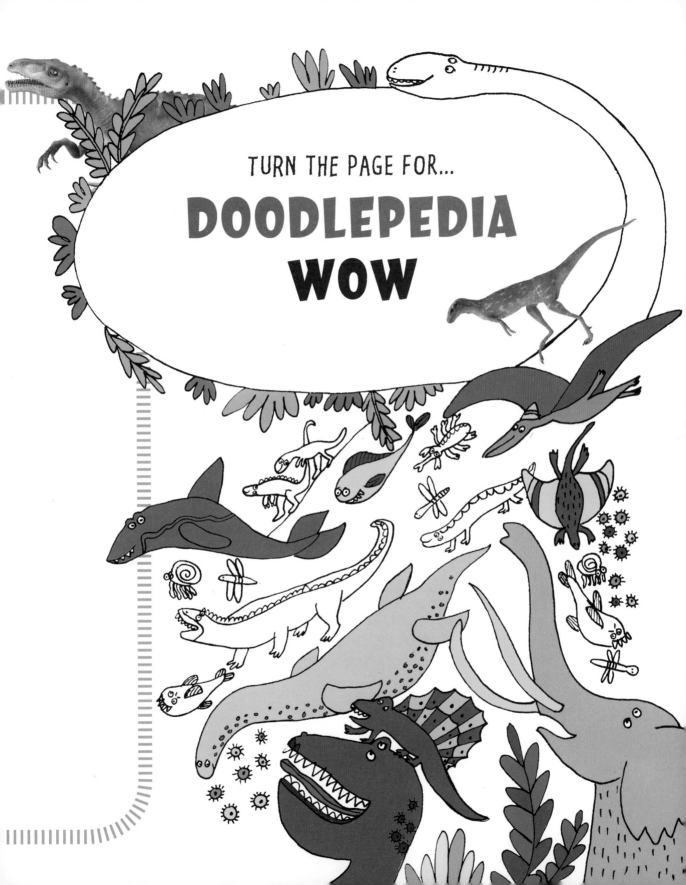

TURN THE PAGE FOR...

DOODLEPEDIA
WOW

DOODLEPEDIA
WOW

The race is on!

Car racing is fast and exciting. The cars that compete in Formula 1 can reach speeds of up to 225 mph (360 kph)! To make the cars safe, controllable, and fast, the engineers use the science of **aerodynamics**. A Formula 1 car is designed so the air that travels over and past it doesn't slow the car down too much. A Formula 1 car travels fast enough to take off like an airplane, so it also uses the pressure of the air flowing over it to keep it firmly on the track. This **downforce** allows the tires to grip the ground and gives the car more control.

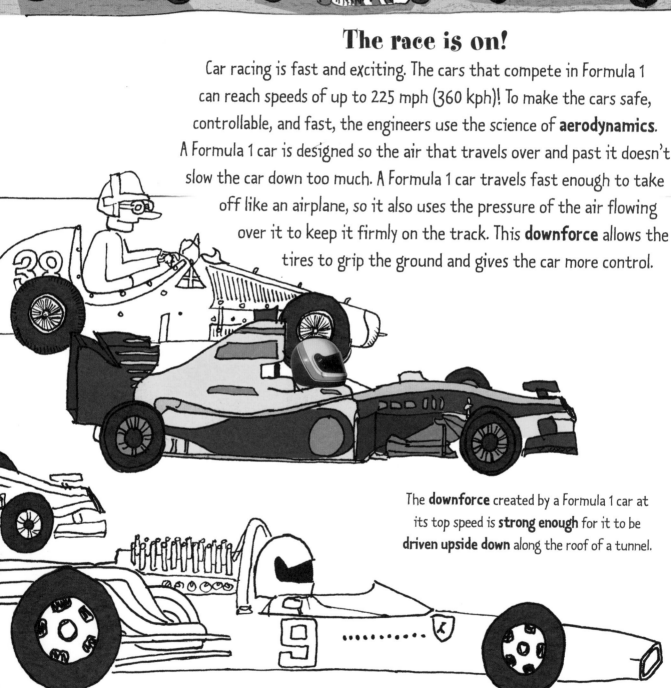

The **downforce** created by a Formula 1 car at its top speed is **strong enough** for it to be **driven upside down** along the roof of a tunnel.

DESIGN A WINNING, SUPERFAST **RACE CAR!**

Check your bags!

All luggage that is going on a plane has to be put through an airport **X-ray scanner**, which displays an image of what is inside each bag. The scanner operators are looking for **dangerous items**, such as weapons and other illegal things, but they must get to see some weird and wonderful things hidden in people's bags!

DRAW WHAT THE **SCANNER** HAS SPOTTED IN THE **LUGGAGE**.

Phones, cameras, and other **solid objects** are the easiest things to spot on the scanner. Luckily, your smelly socks are just a **shadowy outline** in the background.

One suitcase that was left behind at a US airport was found to contain a complete **suit of armor!**

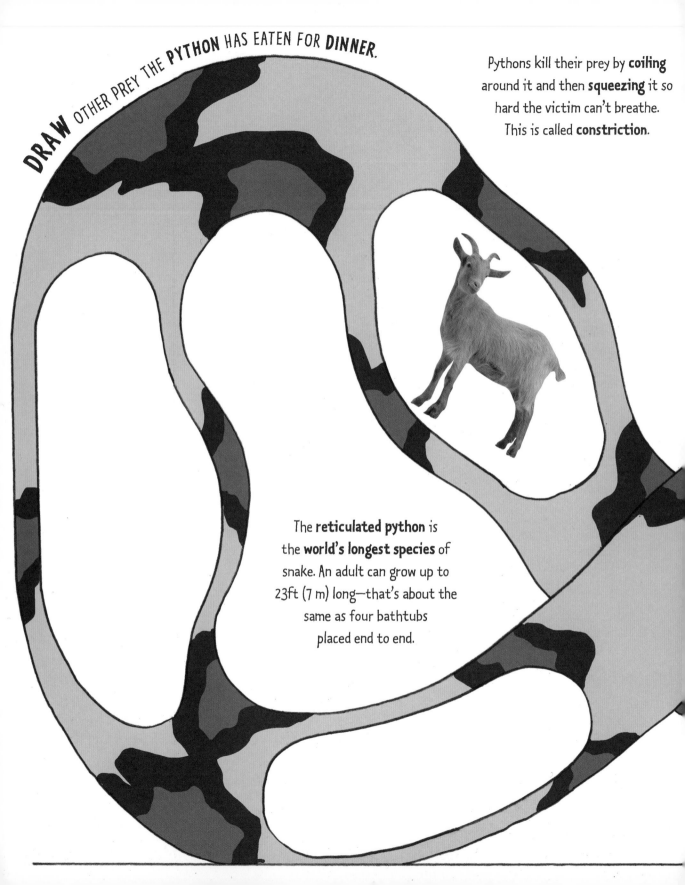

Pythons kill their prey by **coiling** around it and then **squeezing** it so hard the victim can't breathe. This is called **constriction**.

The **reticulated python** is the **world's longest species** of snake. An adult can grow up to 23ft (7 m) long—that's about the same as four bathtubs placed end to end.

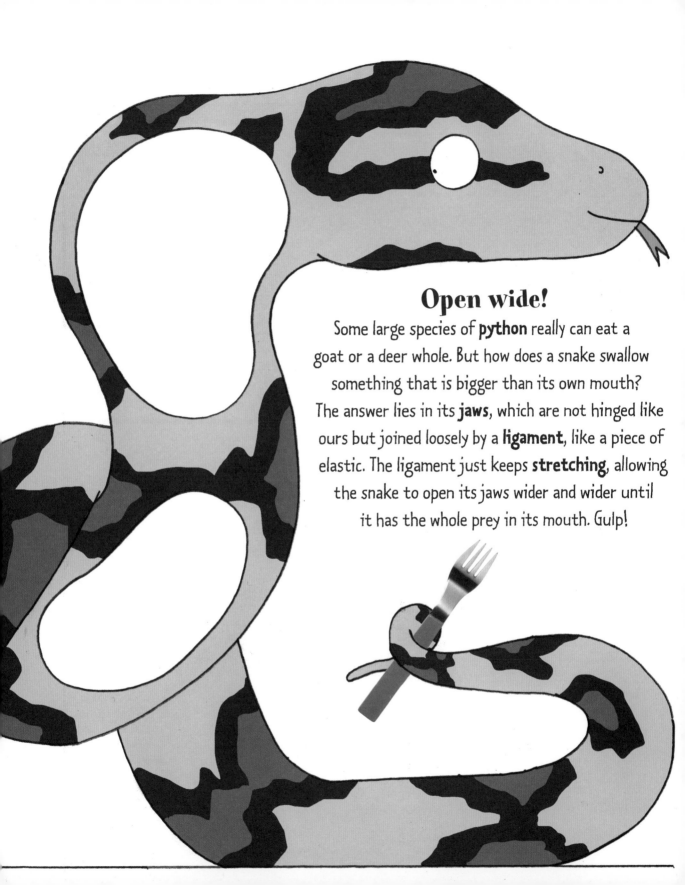

Open wide!

Some large species of **python** really can eat a goat or a deer whole. But how does a snake swallow something that is bigger than its own mouth? The answer lies in its **jaws**, which are not hinged like ours but joined loosely by a **ligament**, like a piece of elastic. The ligament just keeps **stretching**, allowing the snake to open its jaws wider and wider until it has the whole prey in its mouth. Gulp!

Surf's up!

Surfing is difficult and dangerous, but it's lots of fun! The trick is to hop onto the **surfboard** just before the wave **breaks** and then ride along the rolling wall of water. The best **surf waves** start miles out to sea. Storms create **huge ripples** in the water that spread in all directions as waves. They may take days or even weeks to reach land. The waves break when they reach the beach because the shallow water makes the wave grow taller and taller—until it topples over.

DRAW MORE SURFERS AND **DESIGN** YOUR OWN SURFBOARDS.

Big-wave surfing involves waves more than 20 ft (6 m) high. Extreme surfers have ridden waves 70 ft (21 m) high—that's as tall as a seven-story building!

Now wash your hands!

Viruses are a particularly nasty type of germ. They are very, very small—in fact, **millions** can fit on a pinhead only 2 mm wide! They can't survive for very long on their own, but once **inside the cells** of a living thing, such as a plant, animal, or person, they can grow and **reproduce** very fast, making people feel very sick.

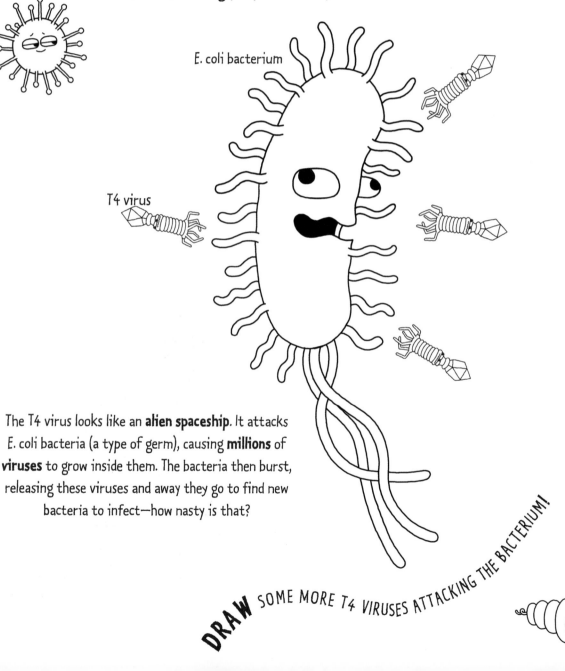

E. coli bacterium

T4 virus

The T4 virus looks like an **alien spaceship**. It attacks E. coli bacteria (a type of germ), causing **millions** of **viruses** to grow inside them. The bacteria then burst, releasing these viruses and away they go to find new bacteria to infect—how nasty is that?

DRAW SOME MORE T4 VIRUSES ATTACKING THE BACTERIUM!

DRAW AND COLOR SOME MORE VIRUSES.

Most **viruses** are between
5–300 nanometers (nm) long.
Considering that a nanometer is
1,000,000,000th of a meter,
that is pretty small!

The **Coup de Monde** is given the winners of the **FIFA World Cup**.

This **spiral** trophy is given to the winner of the **Giro d'Italia** bicycle stage race.

Giro d'Italia

It's a winner!

Nothing beats coming **first** in a sport and winning a **trophy**! In ancient times, winners at sporting events were often awarded a **silver goblet**. The tradition continues to this day, with **giant gold** and **silver trophies** given to **winning athletes and teams** in many major tournaments. To crown their moment of **glory**, winners may hold their trophy aloft and revel in the crowd's **cheers and applause**.

DESIGN SOME SHINY MEDALS.

DESIGN YOUR OWN WINNER'S TROPHY.

Medals are awarded at the **Olympic Games** to **athletes** who finish first, second, or third in their event final.

We need a hero!

HELP!!! The evil villain, cunningly disguised as a burglar, is making off with all the loot. Who can stop him? **Comic strips** like this one have been **entertaining** people since they were first published in 19th-century **newspapers**. Some of the most-loved characters are **superheroes**, such as Batman, Superman, and the Incredible Hulk.

Oh, no! A dastardly robber has taken a valuable painting...

HELP! WE NEED A SUPERHERO!

... but your superhero is here to help! Let's go get that cunning crook!

DRAW YOUR OWN SUPERHERO AND **FINISH** THE STORY.

"Hmm. Here's a clue that will lead me to the stolen painting..."

"... This is a great time to test out my new superhero gadget."

"Got you at last! Stop struggling, you scoundrel!." POW! CRASH! CRUNCH!

"It's off to the jail cell for you! Handcuff him!"

THE END!

COLOR THE MISCHIEVOUS SWINGING MONKEYS.

Baby spider monkeys travel everywhere by keeping a **tight grip** on their mothers, especially when Mom is **hanging upside down.**

Spider monkeys don't have any **thumbs**, but still have a powerful grip.

Hanging around!

Spider monkeys spend all day **hanging** around in the rainforests of South America. They are incredibly **agile**, swinging from branch to branch in search of their favorite foods, which include fruits, seeds, birds' eggs, and insects. They get their name from their **long, spidery arms and legs**. Their **tails** are longer than their bodies and they can use them like an extra limb. This allows them to use their hands and feet for feeding while keeping a **firm grip** on a branch using only their tails.

Mask of art!

African tribal masks can look strange, scary, and fantastic. They have been a part of tribal life in Africa for thousands of years and are still used today in **dances, rituals, and ceremonies**. The **skill** of making the tribal masks is handed down from father to son and the **mask-maker** is given a special role in the tribe. The masks are usually based on human faces, but aren't very realistic.

Some masks are **sacred** and are thought to possess **magical powers**.

Tribal mask makers would use materials that were close to hand, like **wood, stone, and ivory** (animal tusks). The masks were painted using **local dyes** from **plants and soil**.

DESIGN YOUR OWN TRIBAL MASK.

Down under in Australia!

When the first European **explorers** set out to map **Australia**, they had no idea what hideous **hazards** lay ahead. The middle part of the country, called the **Outback**, turned out to be a vast, **desertlike plain**, with **baking temperatures** and very **little water**. Many explorers died there from thirst, hunger, and disease. The wildlife was not always friendly either—the Outback contains some of the worlds' most **poisonous snakes** and **spiders**.

DRAW THE EXPLORERS' CAMPSITE AND **ADD** MORE HAIRY CAMELS AND SLITHERING SNAKES.

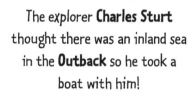

The explorer **Charles Sturt** thought there was an inland sea in the **Outback** so he took a boat with him!

The **wild camels** living in the Outback are **descendants** of camels that **escaped** from early explorations.

Goal!

Soccer is the most popular sport on the planet, with an **incredible 3.5 billion fans worldwide**—that's more than half the world's population! The rules of the modern game were drawn up in Cambridge, England, in 1863, but soccer was **invented more than 2,000 years ago in China**. It caught on in England about 800 years ago, before being **banned for 300 years** after games got too violent. Today, soccer is played in **every country** in the world.

DRAW MORE PLAYERS AND MAKE A WHOLE TEAM.

Whistles were introduced to soccer in 1878, but the **yellow and red cards** were not used until the 1970 World Cup in Mexico.

The **first-ever World Cup** took place in Uruguay in 1930, and **80,000 people watched** the match.

Blast off!

Outer space is only 60 miles (100 km) away, but it's uphill all the way! To get there you need the incredible power of a **rocket**. Built like gigantic fireworks, rockets are pushed upward at high speed by the force of the exhaust fumes from burning fuel being pushed out of its nozzles. Rockets reached space for the first time in 1957, and the **first astronaut** was a Russian **dog** named Laika.

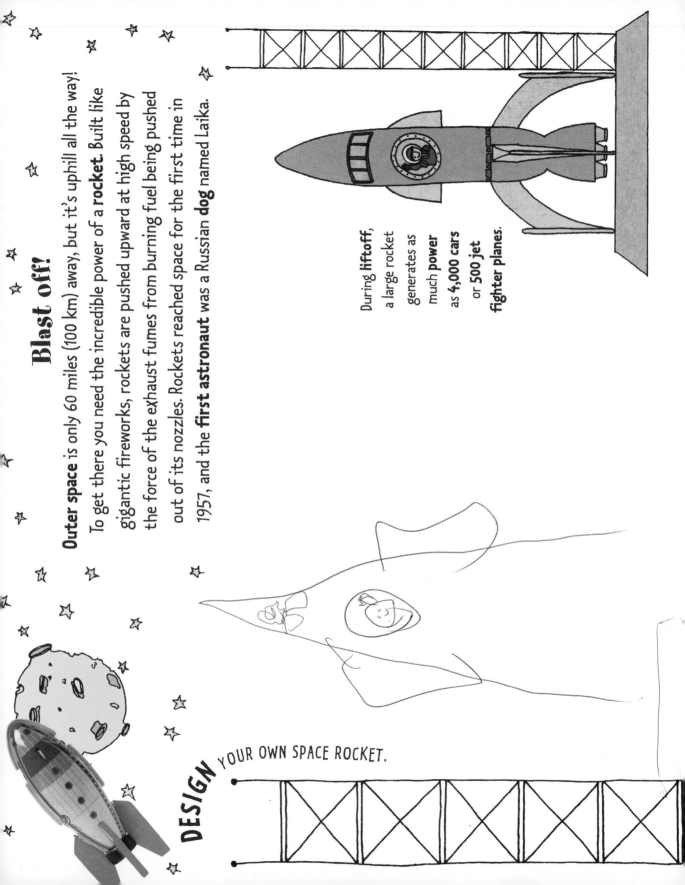

During **liftoff**, a large rocket generates as much **power** as **4,000 cars** or **500 jet fighter planes**.

DESIGN YOUR OWN SPACE ROCKET.

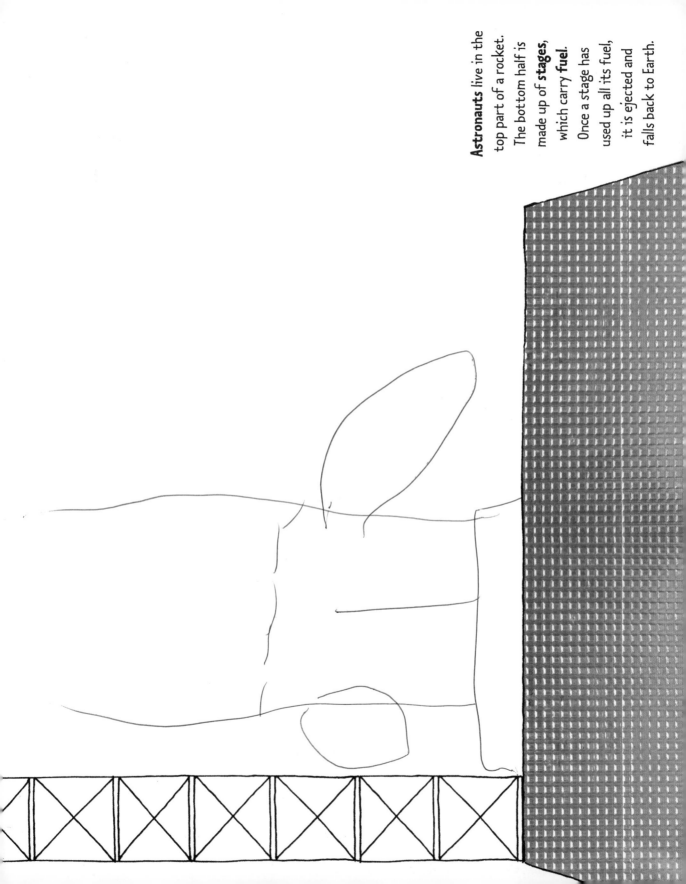

Astronauts live in the top part of a rocket. The bottom half is made up of **stages**, which carry **fuel**. Once a stage has used up all its fuel, it is ejected and falls back to Earth.

Toxic jumpers!

These rainforest-dwelling **amphibians** look colorful and friendly, but they are more **dangerous** than they seem. The bright patterns on the back of a poison dart frog tell predators not to eat it because it is **poisonous**. Rainforest tribes use the frogs's poison on the tips of their **blowpipe darts** when they hunt for food.

One, two, three... jump!

Imagine sitting by an open door of a plane 2.5 miles (4 km) up and being told to jump—scary! For the first 60 seconds you're on your own, free-falling through the sky at speeds of 120 to 180 mph (190 to 290 kph). At 0.5 mile (760 m) above the ground it's time to open your parachute. You'll land in six to seven minutes, so be prepared!

Some say **skydiving** feels like **flying** rather than falling. If you are a beginner, you can **"tandem skydive,"** strapped to an instructor.

Experienced skydivers take part in brief, **death-defying** aerial displays. In 2008, **400 skydivers** joined up for 4 seconds to form a **spiral shape**— a free-fall formation **world record**!

DRAW AND **COLOR** SOME MORE SKYDIVERS.

Glass can be formed when a stroke of **lightning** hits sand.

DESIGN YOUR OWN WACKY GLASS SCULPTURES.

Sandy glass!

Did you know that **glass** is made of **sand**? Sand and other **chemicals** are mixed together, then **heated** to an extremely **high temperature**. The mixture melts and becomes a thick liquid. While it is **cooling** it can be bent into different shapes or poured out flat to make windows and mirrors. **Glass sculptures** can be made by twisting and stretching the glass into all sorts of shapes, and adding other pieces of **colored glass** so that it all sticks together as it cools.

It's cold out there!

Life can get **very chilly** in the Arctic regions around the **North Pole**, especially in the winter. The **animals** that live there have special adaptations to help them live with the cold. Most have a **fur coat** or lots of feathers to help them **keep warm**. A type of **Arctic fish** has a special protein in its blood that stops it from **freezing solid**. Some animals spend many months asleep in **dens and burrows** when food gets scarce. Others go on long journeys **to escape** the bad weather and search for food.

DRAW SOME MORE ANIMALS ON THE ICE.

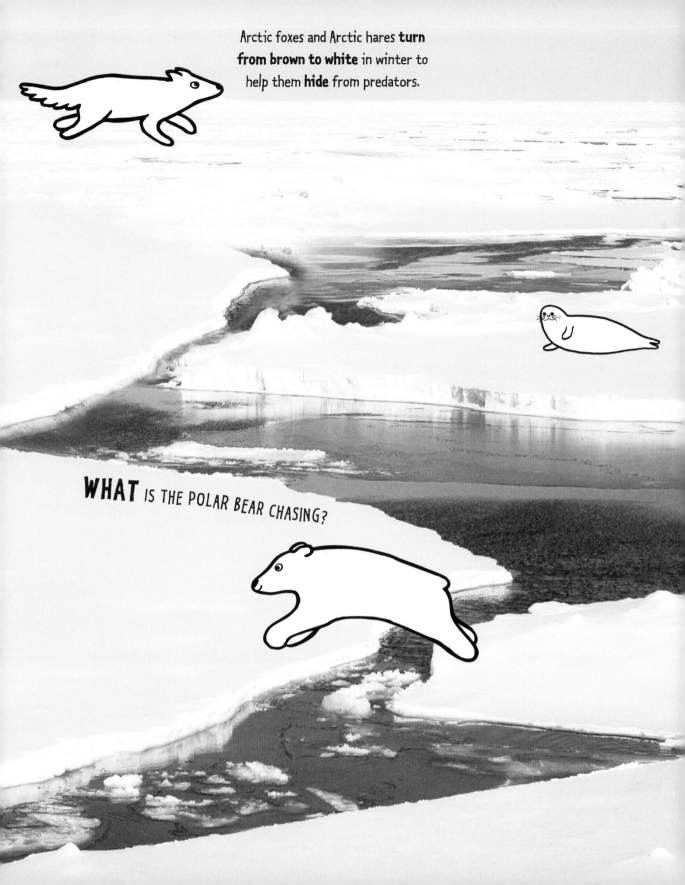

Arctic foxes and Arctic hares **turn from brown to white** in winter to help them **hide** from predators.

WHAT IS THE POLAR BEAR CHASING?

Insects galore

Some **900,000** different kinds of living insect have been identified and named, but scientists believe that there are still many more out there that have yet to be discovered. Some say there could be more than **30 million** different kinds of insect in total!

It's been estimated that there are 10 quintillion individual insects alive at any one time — that's **a 10 with 18 zeros** after it!

Approximately **80%** of all the animal species in the world are insects!

DRAW SOME MORE INSECTS
AND CREATE A **BUG FEST**!

Earth's gravity still has an effect on people in space—just not as much. If a **ladder connected** Earth and a **spacecraft in orbit**, and you climbed up it, you would **weigh 11% less** at the top! So if you weigh 60 lb (27 kg), you'd only weigh about 53 lb (24 kg) at the top of the ladder.

Floating in space

Did you know that **astronauts are not really weightless**? Instead, they are **just constantly falling** toward Earth, together with the spacecraft and everything inside it. So **why don't they fall out of the sky?** Well, the Earth's surface is curved. As the spacecraft and its contents fall to Earth, they are also **traveling extremely fast "sideways."** The Earth's surface curves away from them as fast as they are falling so they end up **orbiting** the Earth and never reach the surface.

To remain in orbit, the **International Space Station** must travel about 17,500 miles per hour (28,000 km per hour)—now that's fast!

DRAW THE ASTRONAUTS FLOATING AROUND THEIR **SPACE STATION**.

To stop the colossal building from collapsing into the sea, **giant concrete pillars** beneath it descend 80 ft (25 m) below sea level.

Welcome to Australia!

Sydney Opera House is Australia's most famous building and a masterpiece of **modern architecture**. Surrounded by the glittering waters of beautiful **Sydney Harbour**, it resembles a **flotilla of boats**, their white sails filled by the wind. The "sails" consist of 10 vast concrete **shells** covered with **gleaming white and cream tiles**. Inside are **seven halls**, the largest of which contains one of the **world's largest pipe organs**, with more than 10,000 pipes.

There are more than **1 million** glossy white and cream tiles on the roof of the Sydney Opera House.

Greetings from Sydney!

DRAW MORE **BOATS** IN THE **HARBOR**.

DRAW WHAT'S LIVING IN THE ROCKPOOL.

The **Goby Rock fish** has a **suction cup** on its underside, which it uses to **cling** to rocks so it doesn't get **washed away** with the tide.

It's a hard life!

One minute it's **low tide** and the sun is beating down and evaporating water from the **rockpool** shallows, making them saltier than usual; the next minute, it's **high tide**, huge waves are crashing down onto the pools, and the water temperature is dropping. These are the **daily living conditions** that any creature or plant living in a rockpool has to cope with if it is to **survive**.

DRAW SOME MORE SKIERS AND SNOWBOARDERS—WHO WILL BE THE FIRST TO MAKE A JUMP?

Nerves of steel!

Extreme skiing and snowboarding take a lot of **nerve and skill**. An **extreme skier** can reach speeds between 125 and 155 mph (200 and 250 kph), and **extreme snowboarders** have been known to go as fast as 125 mph (200 kph)! Traveling this fast, they have to have their wits about them so they can **dodge obstacles** such as rocks, trees, and crevasses (tricky), **avoid avalanches** (almost impossible!), and be able to complete **amazing jumps** successfully!

Avalanches are incredibly powerful and **destructive**. Slabs of dry snow can reach speeds of 80 mph (129 kph) within 5 seconds of starting their **downward slide**.

DESCRIBE OR **DRAW** A TYPICAL DAY IN YOUR NOTEBOOK.

BURIED BY

....

Spacecraft have even taken time capsules into space for **future space travelers** to find. Voyager 1 and 2 have a gold-plated, copper phonograph record on board, containing pictures and sounds of **life on Earth**. It will take around **40,000 years** before the spacecraft reach another planetary system!

Future treasures!

Have you ever thought about making a **time capsule** and leaving it for people to discover many years from now? Time capsules commonly contain **photos, diaries, and objects** so that future generations can have a **"snapshot"** of what life was like in the past. A time capsule in Nebraska has a **white pyramid** above ground to mark where it is buried. It has around **5,000 items** inside it—including **two cars!**

DRAW WHAT YOU WOULD STORE IN YOUR **TIME CAPSULE.**

It's snowing!

It's always exciting when snow starts to fall. These fluffy **snowflakes** started life as miniscule **crystals of ice**, high up in the clouds. The crystals gradually join together to make heavier six-sided **clusters** that start to fall toward the ground. If the **air temperature** is **cold** enough, the clusters fall to Earth as snowflakes.

COMPLETE THE FALLING SNOWFLAKES.

DRAW SNOWFLAKES OF YOUR OWN.

Snowflakes always have **six branches**, but they come in an endless **variety** of **patterns** and **sizes**. No two snowflakes are ever the same.

Most snowflakes are so **tiny** that we can only see their shapes through a **microscope**. The snow that arrives on the ground is usually groups of flakes clumped together.

Follow *that* termite!

A termite mound is like an iceberg—only a little sticks up and the rest, including **tunnels**, is hidden from view. Made entirely from **termite poop, spit,** and **mud,** the mound can reach 26 ft (8 m) tall and 120 tons (110 metric tons) in weight. Hidden in the maze of tunnels are as many as a **million termite workers** and their **king** and **queen.**

The top part of a termite mound works like a **chimney,** letting warm air escape. This keeps the **temperature** underground **just right.**

FIND THE WAY TO THE **BOTTOM** OF THE **MOUND** AND BACK OUT OF THE **TOP**.

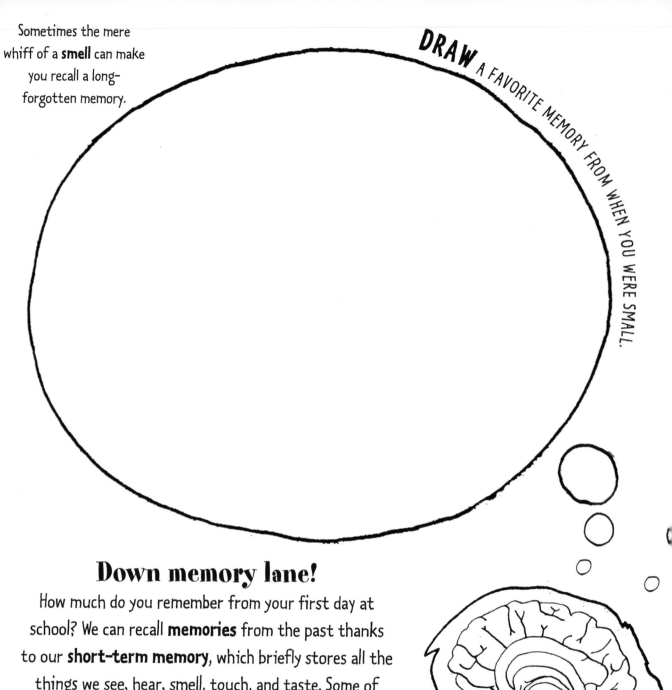

Sometimes the mere whiff of a **smell** can make you recall a long-forgotten memory.

DRAW A FAVORITE MEMORY FROM WHEN YOU WERE SMALL.

Down memory lane!

How much do you remember from your first day at school? We can recall **memories** from the past thanks to our **short-term memory**, which briefly stores all the things we see, hear, smell, touch, and taste. Some of these memories then move to **long-term** storage, allowing us to remember them months or years later.

There isn't just one place in our **brains** where our memories are kept, but a part of the brain, called the **hippocampus**, plays a vital role in turning short-term memories into long-term ones.

Hippocampus

DRAW YOUR EARLIEST MEMORY.

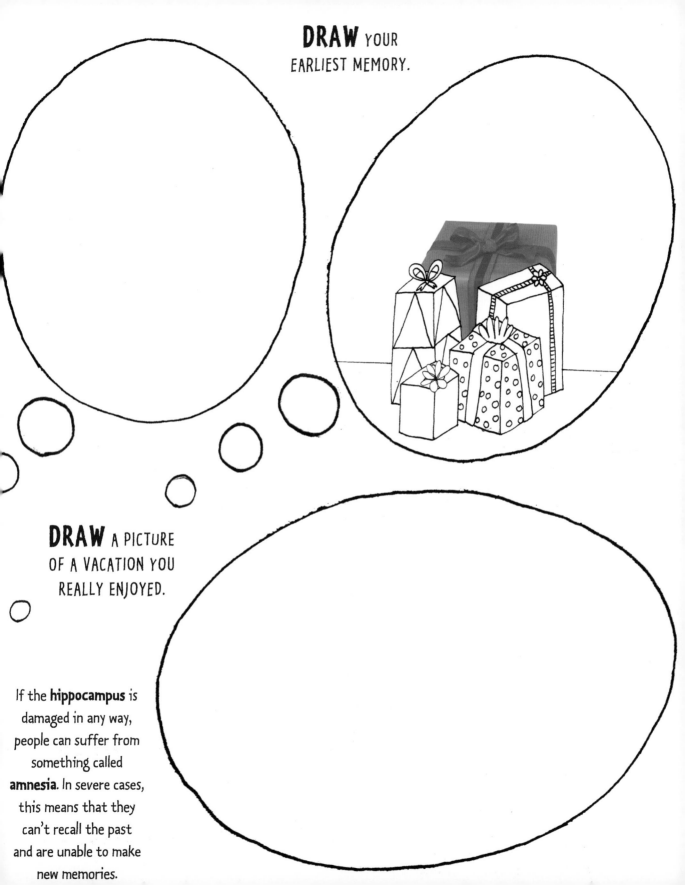

DRAW A PICTURE OF A VACATION YOU REALLY ENJOYED.

If the **hippocampus** is damaged in any way, people can suffer from something called **amnesia**. In severe cases, this means that they can't recall the past and are unable to make new memories.

Gaming world!

Things have certainly changed a lot since the first **video games** were **invented** in the 1970s. Today, the games industry employs thousands of people worldwide and makes more than twice as much money as the movie industry in the US alone. It takes a

Games can be based on **any subject**—sports, cartoons, racing, action adventures, and much, much more.

DESIGN YOUR OWN CONSOLE GAME.

team of up to 50 people to create a **video game**, including programmers, graphic designers, artists, sound designers, musicians, and game testers. Other teams design the **consoles** themselves. So if you love playing video games, this could be the career for you!

The **first handheld electronic game**, *Auto Race*, was launched in 1976. The graphics were very basic— the player's car was just a bright blip on a tiny screen.

Mount Everest is 29,035 ft (8,848 m) tall, and it is **still growing!** Every year it gets a few millimeters higher due to movements of the **Earth's crust.**

On top of the world!

Intrepid **climbers** from all over the world travel to **Nepal** for the ultimate challenge—conquering **Mount Everest**, the **world's tallest mountain**. It's a dangerous climb, so dangerous that the area above 26,000 ft (8,000 m) is known as the **"death zone."** Climbers have to battle with **high winds, subzero temperatures**, and **low oxygen levels**. But it's all worth it for the magic moment when they reach the **summit** and stand on the very top of the world!

DRAW MORE FEARLESS CLIMBERS.

Many climbers who get into difficulties on Everest are **rescued by helicopter**. In 2005, one helicopter set a record for the highest ever landing by touching down on the summit!

The **stripes** are not just fur deep—if you shaved a tiger, the **skin** would be striped underneath, too!

DRAW THE TIGER'S STRIPES.

A tiger's **terrifying**, loud **roar** can be heard as far as 2 miles (3 kilometers) away.

DRAW SOME MORE TIGERS PROWLING THROUGH THE GRASS.

Prowling in the shadows!

Normally an animal's camouflage helps it to hide from predators, but a tiger's **striped skin** helps it to hide from its **prey**. The lines break up the outline of its body, helping the tiger blend into shadows created by the long grass. This means it can **creep up on its victim** without being spotted. A tiger's stripes are as unique as fingerprints are to people; no two tigers have the same pattern.

Our **bodies** are full of chemical reactions. There are more than 100 trillion cells in the human body and **each cell** produces **thousands** of **chemical reactions**. That adds up to quite a lot!

Bubble, fizz, bang!

Everything in the world, in fact, everything in the universe, is made up of stuff, or as the scientists like to call it, **matter**. When **energy**, such as heat, light, or electricity is **added to matter**, changes called chemical reactions can take place—occasionally they can be very **explosive**! Scientists experiment with chemical reactions in **laboratories**, but they happen all around you and inside you, too!

Rotting food is a chemical reaction! **Bacteria** (a germ) and fungi cause irreversible changes in food. They also create quite a **stink**!

Extremely dry!

The **Atacama Desert** in Chile, South America, is a very thirsty place. Situated high in the **Andes Mountains**, some weather stations there have never recorded a **single drop of rain**. The mountains are the reason for this. They are so high that rainclouds coming in from the Pacific Ocean are forced to drop their load of water on the coastal side of the mountains in order to rise over the tops. By the time the clouds have reached the Atacama on the other side, there is practically **no water** left.

Space scientists test their **space robots** in the Atacama Desert, since the **landscape is similar to that of Mars.**

DESIGN YOUR OWN SPACE ROBOT.

ADD SOME MORE **SHAGGY** LLAMAS.

Incredibly wet!

There are several contenders for the title of **wettest inhabited place** on Earth. It all depends on how you measure it. One of them is **Lloró** in Colombia. This town receives 44 ft (13.3 m) of rain spread throughout the year. Another contender is **Mawsynram** in India. This gets 39 ft (11.8 m), although most of this falls during the short **monsoon season**.

Cloudbursts can drop 4 in (10 cm) of rain in an hour.

DRAW HOW YOU WOULD GET ACROSS THE FLOOD.

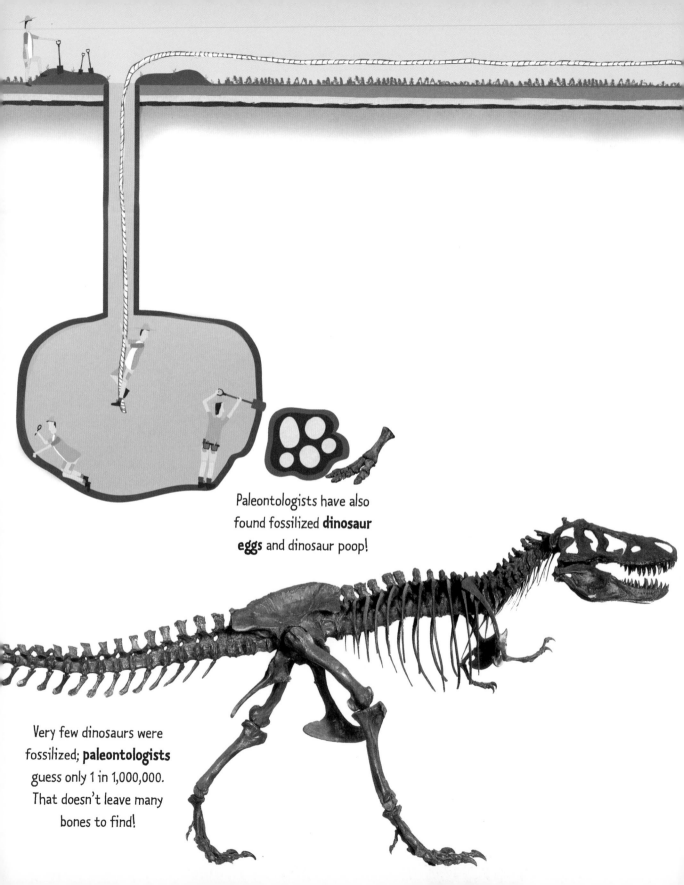

Paleontologists have also
found fossilized **dinosaur
eggs** and dinosaur poop!

Very few dinosaurs were
fossilized; **paleontologists**
guess only 1 in 1,000,000.
That doesn't leave many
bones to find!

Buried bones

Everything we have learned about dinosaurs comes from their **fossilized remains**. Fossils need certain conditions to form. When a dead dinosaur gets covered in sand or mud, its bones are **preserved** and over millions of years the sand and mud turn to rock. The **bones** of the dead dinosaur **absorb** minerals and harden into fossils— ready for dino-seekers (paleontologists) to find them.

DRAW SOME **FOSSILIZED BONES** FOR THE PALEONTOLOGISTS TO DISCOVER.

Viking attack!

If you had lived a thousand years ago, this is something you would not have wanted to see—a boatful of scary **Vikings**! These fierce warriors from **Scandinavia** terrorized people all over Europe, **raiding** their towns and villages, **stealing** anything valuable they could grab, and leaving a trail of **death and destruction** behind them.

A Viking warrior wore a **metal helmet** and carried a **shield**. He was armed with a **sword**, **ax**, or **spear** and was not afraid to use it!

The Vikings crossed the sea in wooden ships, called **longboats**, powered by oars and a sail and decorated with a dragon's head.

DRAW MORE FEARSOME **FIGHTERS** TO COMPLETE THE **VIKING ARMY**.

DRAW AND COLOR MORE BALLOONS!

Up, up, and away!

A **hot-air balloon** may not be the fastest way to travel, but it is probably one of the most amazing! A **burner** under the balloon burns **propane gas**, which **heats the air** inside the balloon. As the air warms up, the balloon **rises**. To go higher, the pilot turns up the **flame**. To stop rising or lose height, he pulls a cord, which opens a **valve** at the top of the balloon and allows some hot air to **escape**.

The **highest** a balloon has ever flown was in 2005 in **Mumbai, India**. It went up 69,852 ft (21,290 meters)—that's 13 miles (21 km) high!

The first **passengers** of the very first hot-air balloon in 1783 were a **sheep**, a **rooster**, and a **duck**!

DESIGN YOUR OWN BALLOON.

Supercool gadgets!

Have you ever wanted to be a **spy**? You'll need some cool gadgets to help you. How about sunglasses with a **hidden camera**, night-vision **goggles** for spying after dark, a voice-activated pen to records conversations, or a **roving robot** that can do the spying for you. What may appear to be a normal everyday object, may in fact be a spy **gadget**, so keep a lookout!

A spy is a person employed to **collect secret information**, known as **"intelligence,"** about another country's government, military, or industries.

DRAW SOME MORE **SNEAKY** SPY GADGETS INSIDE THE CASE.

DESIGN AN ALL-SEEING, ALL-HEARING, COOL SPY ROBOT.

The **largest bats** have a **wingspan**
of more than 5 ft (1.5 m).

DRAW MORE **BATS** FLYING AT NIGHT.

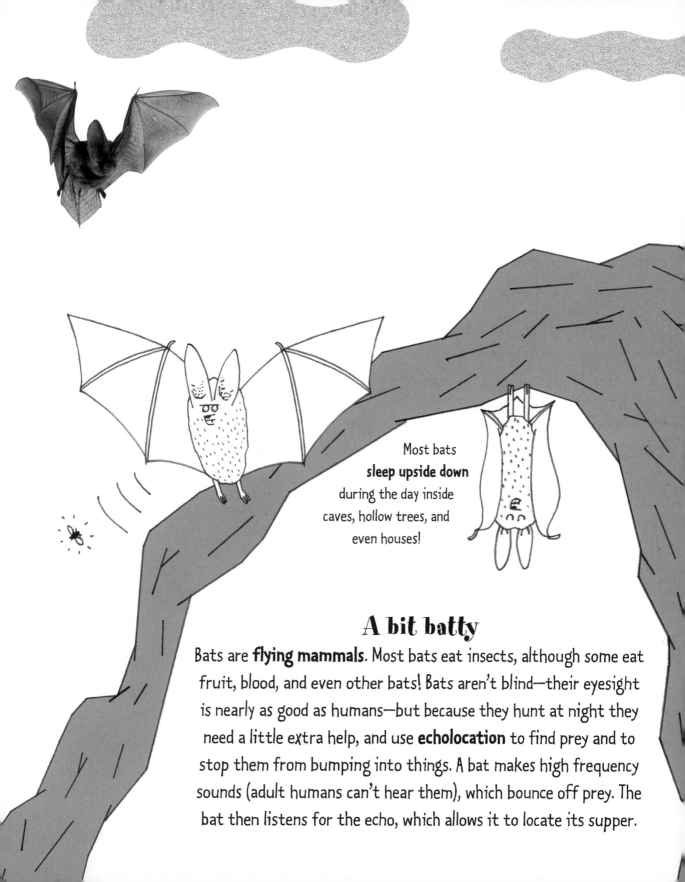

Most bats **sleep upside down** during the day inside caves, hollow trees, and even houses!

A bit batty

Bats are **flying mammals**. Most bats eat insects, although some eat fruit, blood, and even other bats! Bats aren't blind—their eyesight is nearly as good as humans—but because they hunt at night they need a little extra help, and use **echolocation** to find prey and to stop them from bumping into things. A bat makes high frequency sounds (adult humans can't hear them), which bounce off prey. The bat then listens for the echo, which allows it to locate its supper.

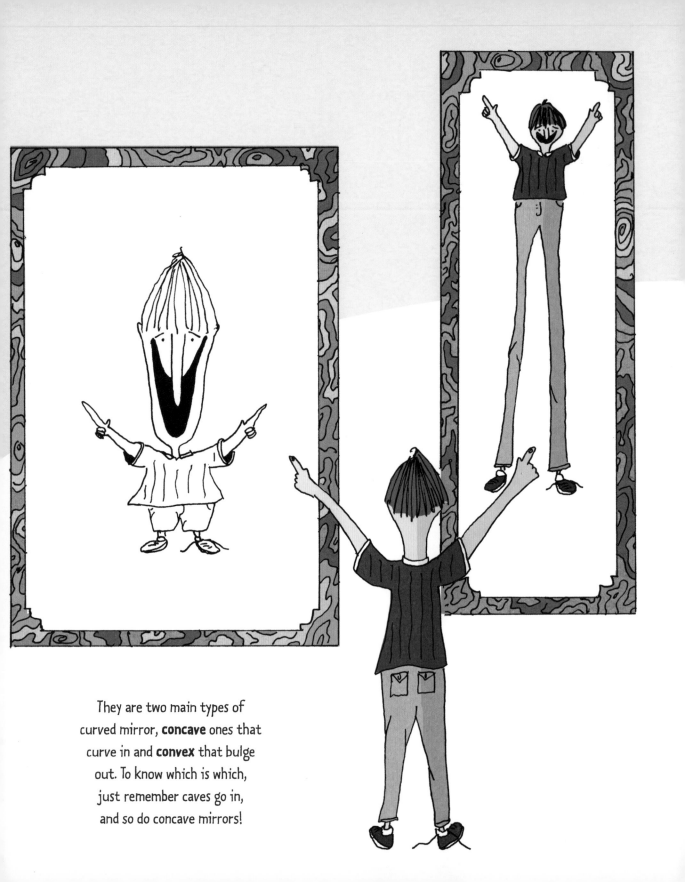

They are two main types of
curved mirror, **concave** ones that
curve in and **convex** that bulge
out. To know which is which,
just remember caves go in,
and so do concave mirrors!

Bendy reflections!

Have you ever been in a **hall of mirrors** at an amusement park or circus?
The mirrors are designed to create **strange and bizarre reflections**.
Some mirrors make you really tall, while others make you really short.
How do the mirrors work? The mirrors **aren't flat** like the ones you have
at home. Instead, they are **warped and curved** so they **reflect** light rays
back at **strange angles**, creating the fun and weird reflections.

The **Burj Khalifa**
elevators travel
at 33 ft (10 m)
a second!

Shanghai World
Finance Center.
1,614 ft (492 m)

Empire State
Building, New York
City. 1,250 ft (381 m)

Burj Khalifa,
Dubai, UAE.
2,716 ft (828 m)

Taipei 101,
Taipei, Taiwan.
1,667 ft (508 m)

Higher and higher and higher...

There have always been **tall buildings**—just think of the **Egyptian pyramids**. However, until the mid-19th century, a building's height was limited by the **number of stairs** people were willing to climb and how much **weight** brick walls could support. Two inventions changed all that—the **elevator** (no more stairs—whoopee!) and the use of a **steel frame** to **support the building**. Since then, buildings have rocketed **skyward**!

The Shard, London, United Kingdom. 1,016 ft (310 m)

Petronas Towers, Kuala Lumpur, Malaysia. 1,482 ft (452 m)

DESIGN YOUR OWN **SKYSCRAPERS**—THE SKY'S THE LIMIT!

Incredibly cold!

Imagine a place where pen ink **freezes** and metal sticks to skin. Welcome to **Oymyakon**, the **coldest inhabited village** on Earth! Situated in **Siberia, Russia**, the temperature here has been known to go as low as −96.16°F (−71.2°C). Winter lasts for **nine months** of the year and children are not allowed outside to play for more than **20 minutes** at a time because the **extreme cold** could damage their lungs.

Strangely enough, Oymyakon is named after a nearby **hot spring!**

DRAW YOURSELF AND YOUR FRIENDS PLAYING OUTSIDE—WRAP UP WARMLY!

Extremely hot!

Dallol in Ethiopia currently holds the record for the world's **highest average temperature**. Most days the thermometer reaches 94°F (34°C), but it can go as high as 148°F (64°C) in the summer. Only a few people live here—it's miles from anywhere, there are no real roads, and abandoned cars that have broken down are still awaiting recovery! The only reliable transportation is a camel.

The landscape is brightly colored red, yellow, and white from the mineral salts that evaporate from **volcanic springs** underground.

COLOR THE LANDSCAPE IN REDS, YELLOWS, AND WHITE.

DRAW SOME REALIBLE CAMELS.

It took the **crew** of a steam train nearly **three hours** to generate enough steam to get the train moving.

DRAW THE MISSING WAGON—WHAT'S INSIDE THEM ALL?

All aboard!

The first trains were called **steam trains** because they were **powered** by steam and belched out great clouds of **steam** and **smoke**. The engine car at the front contained a huge **coal fire** that was used to boil water and turn it into steam, which then traveled through pipes and pushed **pistons** (rods) that turned the wheels around. Steam engines generated fantastic power—enough to pull a long row of heavy cars.

DESIGN YOUR OWN TRAIN.

Terrors from the deep!

Life on Earth most likely started in **the oceans**. There are **millions of species** of animal that live in the oceans, some we haven't yet discovered because the oceans are so **vast and very, very deep**. Some of the fish that live in the oceans are very **strange and unique**.

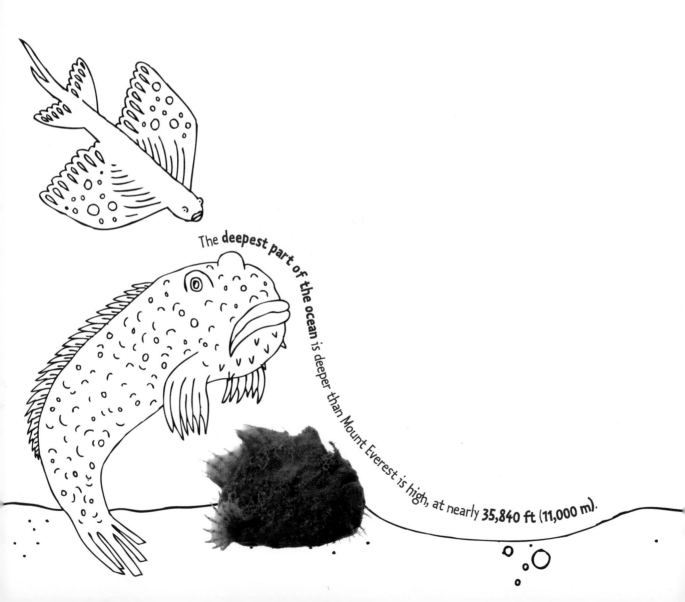

The **deepest part of the ocean** is deeper than Mount Everest is high, at nearly **35,840 ft (11,000 m)**.

DRAW MORE TERRORS FROM THE DEEP.

Deep, deep down it is completely dark. Many deep-sea creatures give out a ghostly blue light, called bioluminescence, so they can find food and mates.

The **longest known** cave system, **Mammoth Cave** in Kentucky, has more than **390 miles (628 km)** of interconnecting **passages**.

Water dripping **down** from the roofs of some caves leaves behind tiny amounts of the **mineral calcite**, which gradually form a **stalactite**. A **stalagmite grows up** where water drips on to the cave floor.

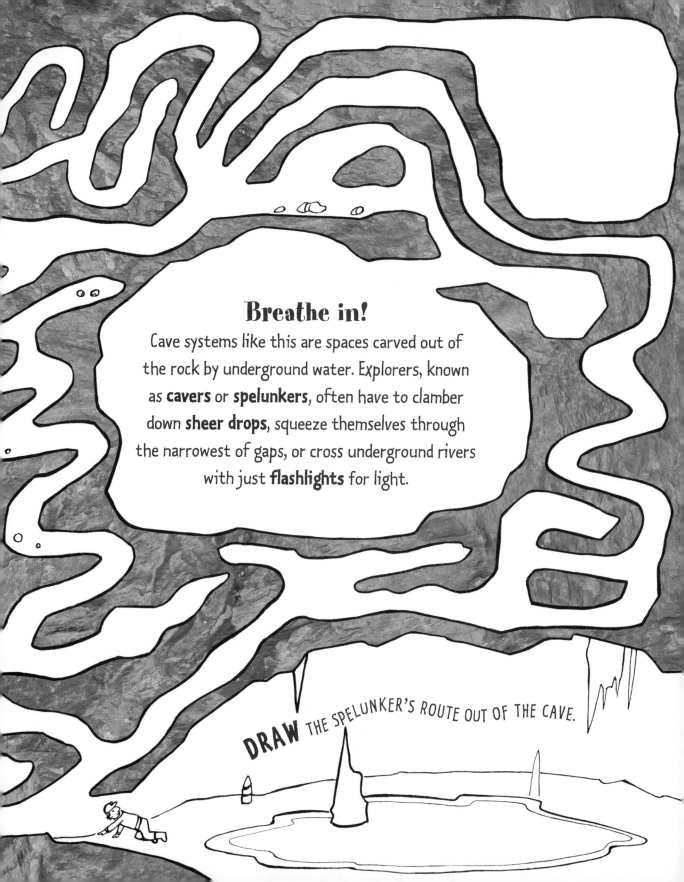

Breathe in!

Cave systems like this are spaces carved out of the rock by underground water. Explorers, known as **cavers** or **spelunkers**, often have to clamber down **sheer drops**, squeeze themselves through the narrowest of gaps, or cross underground rivers with just **flashlights** for light.

DRAW THE SPELUNKER'S ROUTE OUT OF THE CAVE.

In the **future**, there will need to be rules about driving the **sky highways**—you can't paint yellow lines or have median strips up there!

COMPLETE THIS CAR SO THAT IT CAN FLY HIGH!

DESIGN
YOUR OWN FLYING
CAR—HOW FAST
CAN IT GO?

Curtiss Autoplane 1917

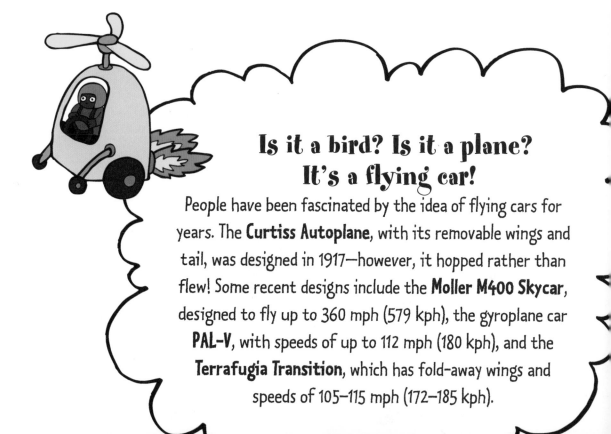

Is it a bird? Is it a plane?
It's a flying car!

People have been fascinated by the idea of flying cars for years. The **Curtiss Autoplane**, with its removable wings and tail, was designed in 1917—however, it hopped rather than flew! Some recent designs include the **Moller M400 Skycar**, designed to fly up to 360 mph (579 kph), the gyroplane car **PAL-V**, with speeds of up to 112 mph (180 kph), and the **Terrafugia Transition**, which has fold-away wings and speeds of 105–115 mph (172–185 kph).

The leaves these ants are carrying won't be eaten. Instead, the ants **munch the leaves** up and **mix them** with their saliva. The ants then eat the **fungus** that grows on the mixture.

COMPLETE AND **COLOR** THE LINE OF ANTS.

As strong as an...ant?

A ¹/₃-inch- (1-cm-) long **leaf-cutter ant** can climb 100-ft (30-m) trees, cut off pieces of leaf (which can weigh 50 times its body weight), then, following a special scent trail, **carry** these back to its **underground nest**. Imagine the equivalent for you—it would mean walking several miles with a medium-sized van on your back!

An **ant's nest** can be the size of a **small car**!

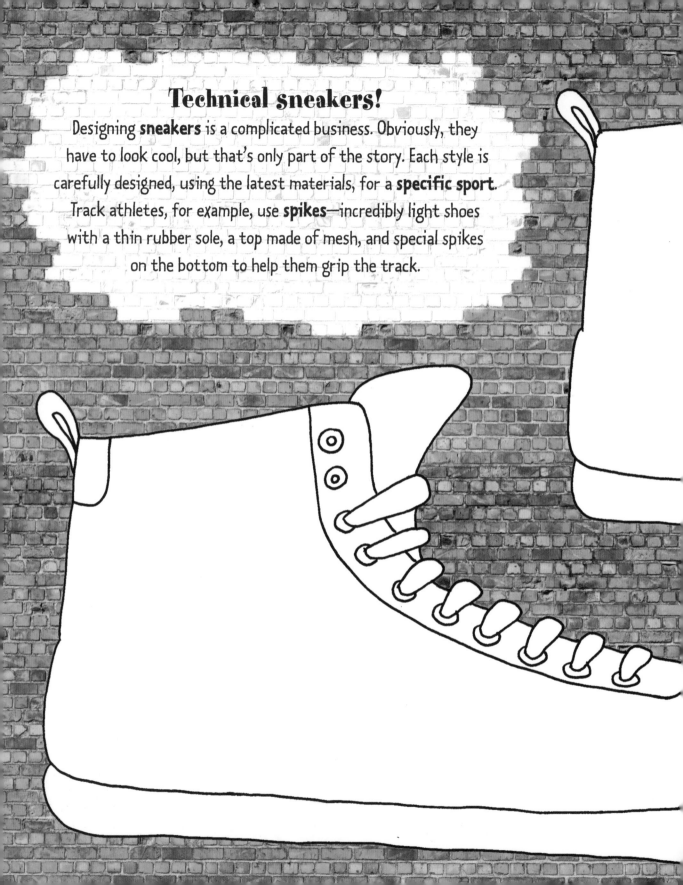

Technical sneakers!

Designing **sneakers** is a complicated business. Obviously, they have to look cool, but that's only part of the story. Each style is carefully designed, using the latest materials, for a **specific sport**. Track athletes, for example, use **spikes**—incredibly light shoes with a thin rubber sole, a top made of mesh, and special spikes on the bottom to help them grip the track.

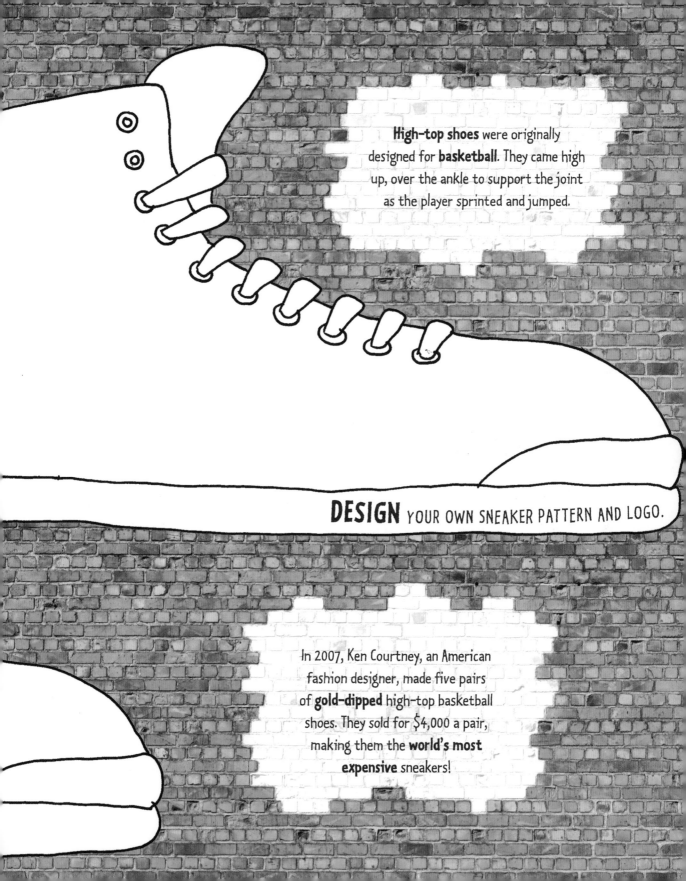

High-top shoes were originally designed for **basketball**. They came high up, over the ankle to support the joint as the player sprinted and jumped.

DESIGN YOUR OWN SNEAKER PATTERN AND LOGO.

In 2007, Ken Courtney, an American fashion designer, made five pairs of **gold-dipped** high-top basketball shoes. They sold for $4,000 a pair, making them the **world's most expensive** sneakers!

The United Kingdom has the most CCTV cameras per citizen, with 4.2 million cameras—that's **one CCTV camera for every 15 people!**

DRAW WHAT IS HAPPENING ON THE MONITORS.

According to statistics, a person can be caught on camera up to **300 times** a day!

They're watching you!

Video cameras are used around the world to help us watch and observe. These video cameras form a system called **Closed-circuit television (CCTV)**. CCTV cameras are used for different reasons, from **protecting valuables and property**, observing the public, and even in factories to **monitor procedures** that are too dangerous for humans to be near. CCTV is used to **prevent crimes**, but it is also seen as an **invasion** of people's **privacy**.

What's up there?

If you look up into a clear **night sky**, it's amazing how many different things you can see. Using just your eyes or a telescope, you can spot **the Moon**, hundreds of **stars**, and sometimes even a **shooting star**. Look for **planets** such as Venus or Jupiter, too. Planets are much closer to us than the stars, so they look like **small, bright disks** in the sky. You may also see some **slow-moving** specks of light. These are man-made **satellites** that circle our planet.

A **shooting star** is not really a star at all, but a **meteor**. It is a lump of rock or other debris from space that burns up as it enters the Earth's **atmosphere**.

The easiest **satellite** to spot is the **International Space Station**, because it is very big. It completes an **orbit** of the Earth every 90 minutes. It is often mistaken for a **UFO!**

Giant wheels!

Monster trucks are normal **pickup-style trucks** that have been **customized** with **beefed-up engines** and **giant tires**. Monster trucks are powerful so they can drive over obstacles, such as dirt ramps and normal road cars. Monster trucks can be up to 12 ft (3.5 m) high—that's as high as you, with two of your friends standing on your shoulders! With **giant wheels** and lots of crazy stunts, the monster trucks need really big and **powerful suspensions**, but even then it's a bumpy ride!

Monster trucks are customized in lots of different ways, ranging from colorful patterns to sculpted dinosaur designs!

A new set of giant tires can cost around $12,500—that's a lot of allowance money!

DESIGN YOUR OWN MEGA MONSTER TRUCKS!

DRAW SOMETHING
FANTASTIC
TO FINISH THE SECTION.

DOODLEPEDIA
ANIMAL ANTICS

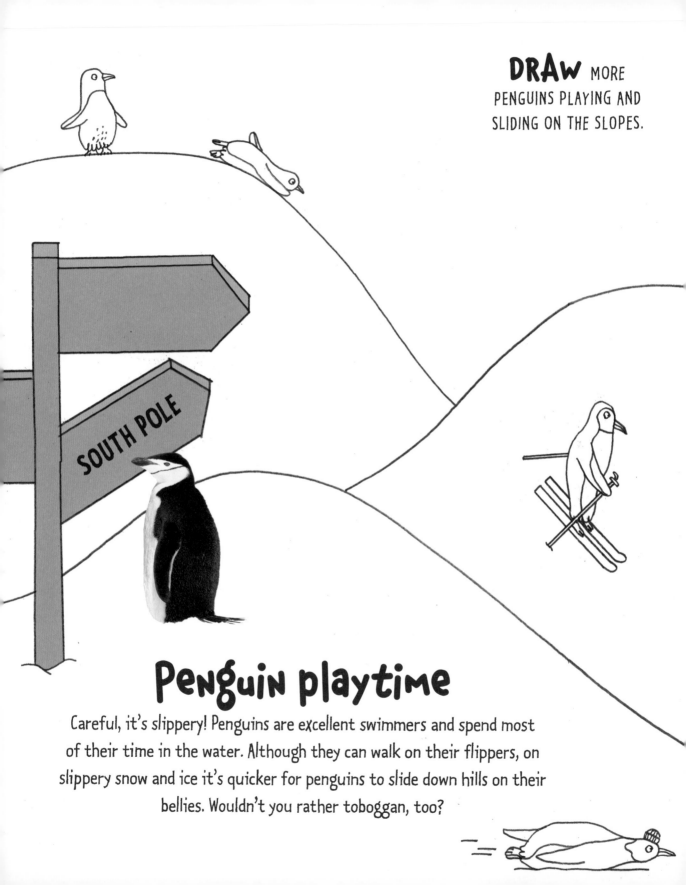

DRAW MORE PENGUINS PLAYING AND SLIDING ON THE SLOPES.

SOUTH POLE

Penguin playtime

Careful, it's slippery! Penguins are excellent swimmers and spend most of their time in the water. Although they can walk on their flippers, on slippery snow and ice it's quicker for penguins to slide down hills on their bellies. Wouldn't you rather toboggan, too?

Adélie Penguins are mostly black with a white front.

Chinstrap Penguins look like they are wearing black hats!

Emperor Penguins are the biggest of all penguins.

COLOR IN THE DIFFERENT KINDS OF PENGUIN.

Penguin moms and dads raise their chicks together.

Chipper chipmunks

Chipmunks sleep underground throughout the cold winter months. But instead of living off stored body fat like many other animals, they gather food in their burrows. They then sleep nearby in their nests, waking every few days to have a snack that keeps them going.

DRAW A SLEEPING CHIPMUNK IN ITS NEST.

FINISH FILLING UP THE HOARD WITH ACORNS.

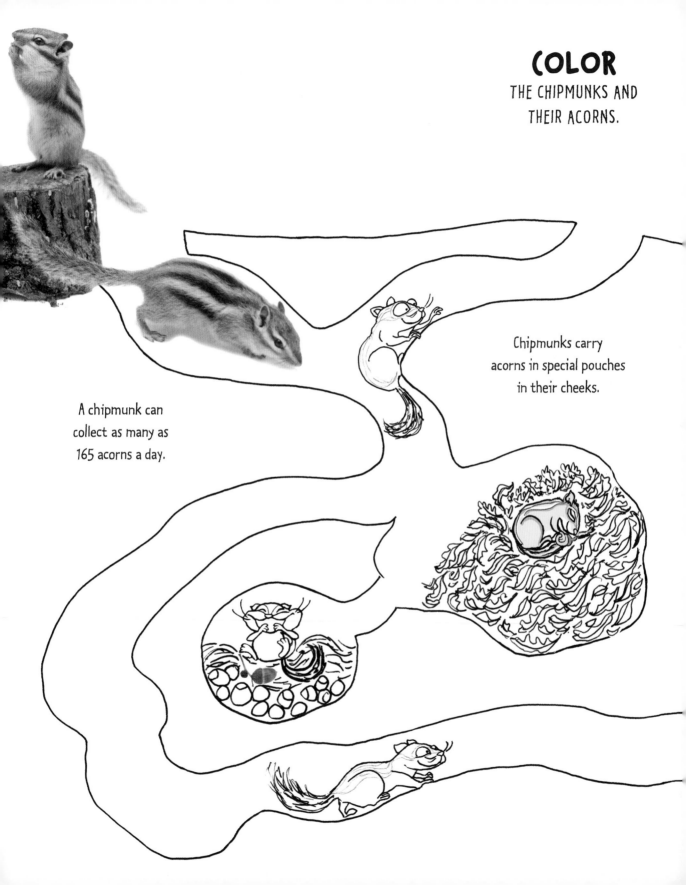

COLOR

THE CHIPMUNKS AND
THEIR ACORNS.

Chipmunks carry
acorns in special pouches
in their cheeks.

A chipmunk can
collect as many as
165 acorns a day.

Pretty polly

Parrot fish have an important job—they keep reefs healthy by scraping away material that builds up on the surface of the coral. However, in doing this, they sometimes break off small pieces of coral. These pass through the intestines of the fish and out the other end as white sand.

DRAW PATTERNS ON THE PARROT FISH.

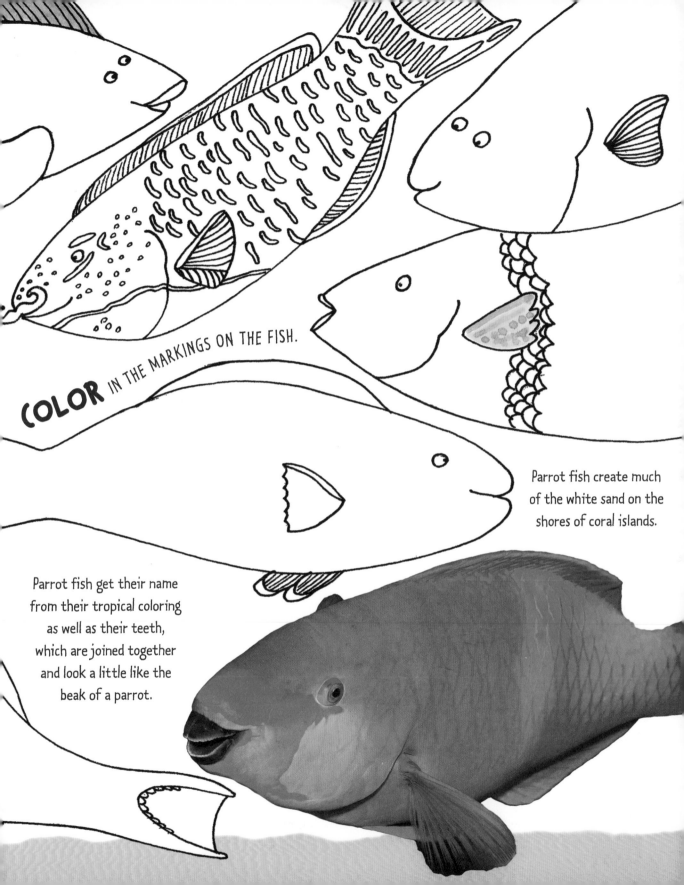

COLOR IN THE MARKINGS ON THE FISH.

Parrot fish create much of the white sand on the shores of coral islands.

Parrot fish get their name from their tropical coloring as well as their teeth, which are joined together and look a little like the beak of a parrot.

Ear, ear!

Elephants are the world's biggest land animals. They can weigh up to 10 tons, or as much as 10 cars! There are three species (types) of elephant: African savanna elephants and African forest elephants live in Africa, and Indian elephants live in Asia. One way to tell them apart is by their ears—African elephants have bigger ears.

Look at this African elephant's ears—they're shaped a little like Africa! On hot days he flaps them to create a cooling breeze.

AFRICA

Indian elephants have smaller ears that are shaped a little like India.

INDIA

DRAW THE EARS ON THE ELEPHANTS TO SHOW WHETHER THEY'RE AFRICAN OR INDIAN.

Spider webs

Spiders make their webs everywhere—in trees, bushes, and even in people's homes. Spiders use their webs to catch insects. Insects either get tangled in the webs or they trip over the threads. This tells the spider to run out and catch the insect. Spiders spin the silk that forms the web. It comes out of openings called spinnerets, located near their rear ends!

Tangle webs can look a little messy!

Spiral orb webs are round in shape.

Funnel webs form a tubelike tunnel.

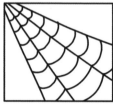

Sheet webs can cover large areas.

DRAW MORE SPIDERS SPINNING WEBS.

Dolphin School

Although dolphins in aquariums often perform amazing tricks like swimming on their tails, dolphins in the wild rarely do. That is, unless someone teaches them how. When a captive bottlenose dolphin was released into the wild off the coast of Australia, scientists were surprised to discover many other dolphins soon performing the same tricks it had learned in captivity. The dolphin had taught its friends!

Dolphins are considered to be among the world's most intelligent animals.

DRAW MORE DOLPHINS PERFORMING THE TRICKS THEY'VE LEARNED.

Bottlenose dolphins get their name from their short, bottlelike beak.

FIND AND COLOR
THE RACCOONS.

COLOR THE MAPLE
LEAVES IN PRETTY
FALL COLORS.

Peekaboo!

Maple trees are found all over the Northern Hemisphere, especially in North America. The large maple leaves turn bright shades of **red** and **gold** in the fall. These forests are full of **wildlife**. One inhabitant is the **raccoon**, a black-and-white **mammal** with a doglike face and a long **bushy tail**. These mischievous animals have a patch of black fur around their eyes that makes them look like masked bandits!

The **largest maple leaf** was found by a boy in Canada. It reached 13 in (36 cm) wide and 11 in (29 cm) in length! That's **three times** as big as your head!

Bowerbird's love nest

To impress a lady, give her... a bit of blue string? It might seem strange to us, but some bowerbird males attract females by building a bower (shelter) and decorating it with blue objects that they've found. And the ladies love it!

Bowerbirds decorate their bowers with man-made objects like pieces of plastic and metal, as well as natural ones such as flowers and feathers.

FEMALE

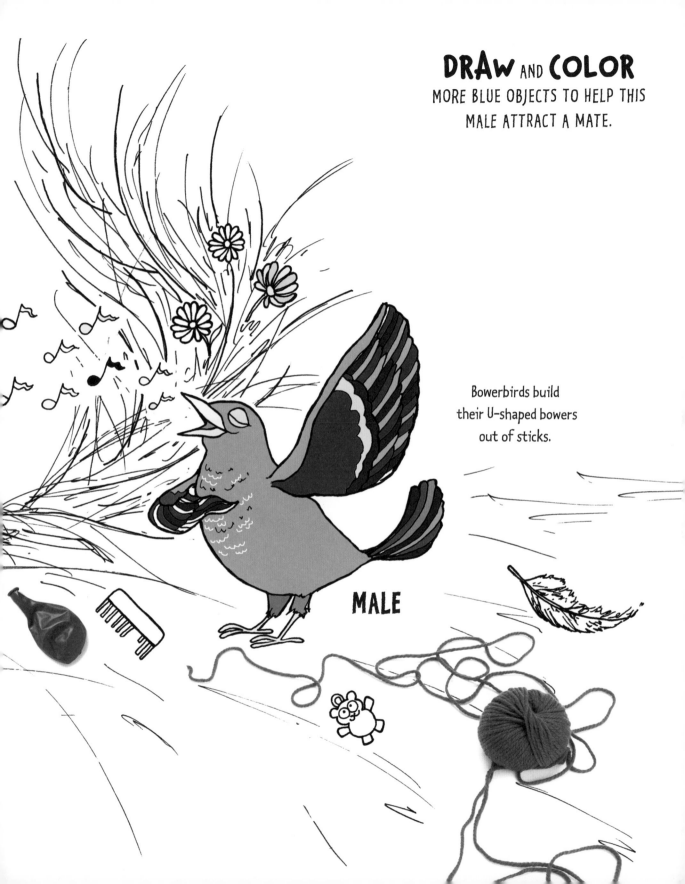

DRAW AND COLOR
MORE BLUE OBJECTS TO HELP THIS MALE ATTRACT A MATE.

Bowerbirds build
their U-shaped bowers
out of sticks.

MALE

Brown bears' feast

Brown bears love salmon and have found a smart way to go fishing. They stand in a river, wait for the fish to swim by, and then grab them in their teeth or paws. Sometimes they even catch salmon leaping out of the water!

Brown bears sleep through the winter, so in the fall, they need to eat lots and lots of food to keep them going during that time.

DRAW MORE SALMON JUMPING OUT OF THE RIVER.

BEWARE OF THE BEARS

Bears sometimes dive in to catch
fish swimming in the water.

DRAW MORE CAPUCHIN MONKEYS BREAKING OPEN FRUIT.

The stone "hammers" used by the capuchins can weigh nearly 4lb (1.7kg)—that's half the monkey's weight!

Young capuchin monkeys learn to break open fruit by watching older monkeys do it. Monkey see, monkey do.

Monkey business

Capuchin monkeys are very smart and know how to break into the hardest fruit. If the fruit is too hard to open using their hands and teeth, they use tools! First, they find somewhere to place the fruit so that it will not move. Then they strike it with a stone to split it open. Dinner is served!

DRAW MORE GECKOS CLIMBING UP AND DOWN THE WINDOW.

Gluey geckos

Do geckos have superpowers? It's easy to think they do, since they can walk up almost any surface, including walls and windows. In fact, their superpower is their specialized feet. The bottoms of their toes are covered in tiny hairlike bumps that can cling to the smallest ridge, allowing the gecko to hang on.

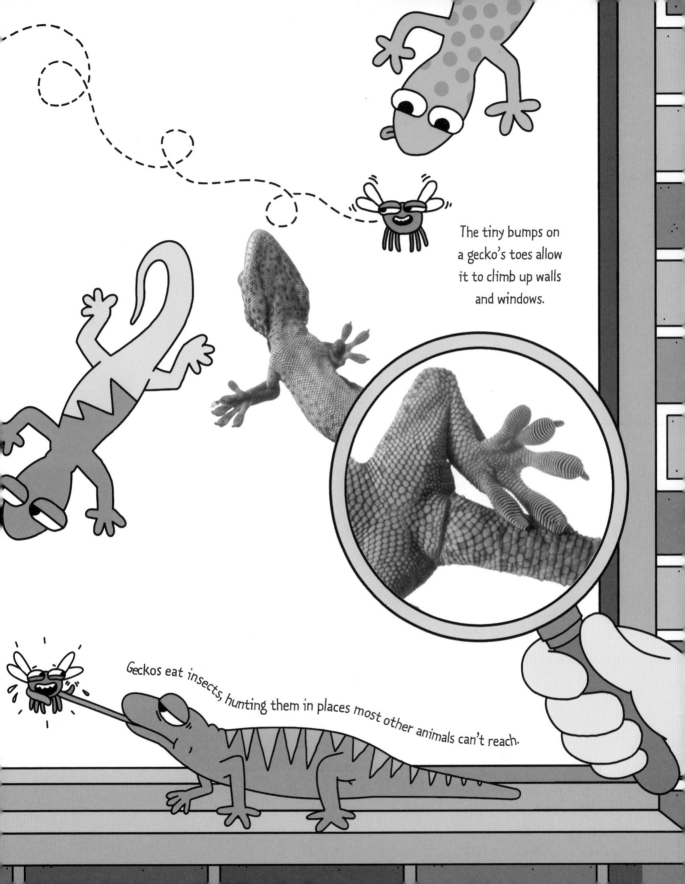

The tiny bumps on a gecko's toes allow it to climb up walls and windows.

Geckos eat insects, hunting them in places most other animals can't reach.

Living on land

Land creatures come in all shapes and sizes. This is no surprise, because the areas of land where they live can be very different. Imagine living in a tropical rainforest, on a high mountaintop, in the frozen Arctic, or in a hot, dry desert. There is one thing all the animals do have in common—each animal is perfectly suited to the place where it lives.

FIND THE CREATURE THAT SHOULDN'T BE ON LAND.

COLOR ALL THE DIFFERENT LAND ANIMALS.

Dressed crab

When they need to hide from predators, dresser crabs know just where to go—to the dress-up box! Dresser crabs can blend in with their surroundings by attaching nearby objects to their bodies. They can do this because they have areas on their shells that stick like Velcro.

DRAW MORE OBJECTS THE DRESSER CRAB CAN USE WHEN IT IS CREATING ITS COSTUMES.

Dresser crabs have been known to wear bits of seaweed, coral, and even sea anemones. How fabulous!

DRAW WHAT THE DRESSER CRAB IS WEARING TO HIDE ITSELF.

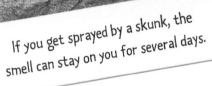
If you get sprayed by a skunk, the smell can stay on you for several days.

DRAW MORE SKUNKS SPRAYING.

You've been Skunked!

Eeeuww, what's that smell? It's worse than rotten eggs—it's a skunk!
When skunks are frightened, they defend themselves by spraying a
strong, horrible scent from a gland under their tails. Before they spray,
skunks give a warning. They stamp their feet and lift up their tails.
Some skunks even do a handstand. You've been warned!

Skunks have very good
aim. They can can hit a target
up to 50ft (15m) away.

Fly fishers

How does a fish hunt for food? With a water pistol, of course! The amazing archerfish catches insects from plants that overhang the water. It knocks them off with a jet of water produced by pressing its tongue against the roof of its mouth and quickly closing its gill covers. It can hit its target from about 5ft (1.5m) away!

DRAW THE WATER SQUIRTS FROM THE FISH TO THE INSECTS.

Archerfish live in streams and lakes in Southeast Asia and northen Australia.

ADD BANDS TO THE FISH AND FINISH COLORING THE PICTURE.

Dancing lemurs

If you ever go down to Madagasgar, you might see lemurs dancing! Most lemurs live in the trees and leap from branch to branch. If the trees are too far apart the lemurs come down and cross the ground with a sideways jump-hop. At the same time, they hold their arms out to the sides so it looks like they're dancing!

Madagascar is an island off the coast of Africa. On our globe, it's colored in red.

DRAW MORE LEMURS DANCING ON THE GROUND.

Can you guess why this is called a
ring-tailed lemur?

Scramble to the sea!

When a **mother sea turtle** is ready to **lay her eggs**,
she swims ashore, and lays and **buries her eggs in a hole**
on a sandy beach. Once she's laid them all, she crawls back
into the sea. After hatching, it may take the **baby turtles**
three or more days to dig their way out of the nest, then it's
a quick **nighttime scramble** down the beach and off to sea!

A baby turtle has a **small horn** on its head, called an **egg-tooth**, which it uses to break out of the egg.

When a baby turtle reaches the water, it **dives** into a wave and **rides** out to sea.

DRAW MORE BABY TURTLES CRAWLING TO THE SEA.

Dung beetle race

All dung beetles deserve a medal. They help keep the planet clean by eating dung (animal poop). Dung beetles known as "rollers" make balls out of dung. They roll the balls to a place where they can be buried to eat later or used as a nest where they lay their eggs. Rollers have to roll their balls quickly or they will be stolen by other dung beetles!

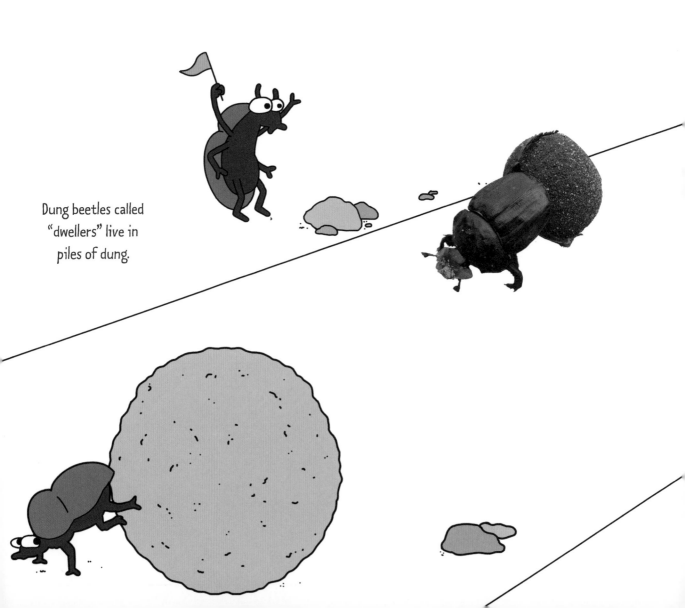

Dung beetles called "dwellers" live in piles of dung.

DRAW MORE DUNG BEETLES IN THE RACE.

Dung beetles can roll a dung ball up to 10 times their weight.

"Tunneler" beetles dig a tunnel under the dung to bury it where they find it.

Stick it out!

Giraffes are excellent at reaching leaves high up in trees. First, because they grow up to 18ft (5.5m) tall—as tall as a two-story building! Second, their very long tongues give them extra reach. A giraffe's tongue can extend to 18in (45cm)—the length of 3 bananas!

Giraffes like to eat acacia leaves. They use their tongues and teeth to strip the leaves from branches.

DRAW MORE GIRAFFES AND THEIR LONG TONGUES.

Each giraffe has a
distinct pattern of patches—
like a fingerprint!

A giraffe's tongue
is this long!

Climbing goats

When people climb mountains, they need all kinds of equipment, such as ropes and axes. When mountain goats do it, they just use their specially shaped hooves. The hooves have a hard outer shell and a rubbery middle that works like a suction cup to grip the ground with every step.

Mountain goats eat plants that grow on the mountains. These include grasses, herbs, and low-growing shrubs.

Mountain goats have a great sense of balance. They can stand on the narrowest ridges.

DRAW A ROUTE UP THE MOUNTAINS FOR EACH OF THE GOATS TO FOLLOW.

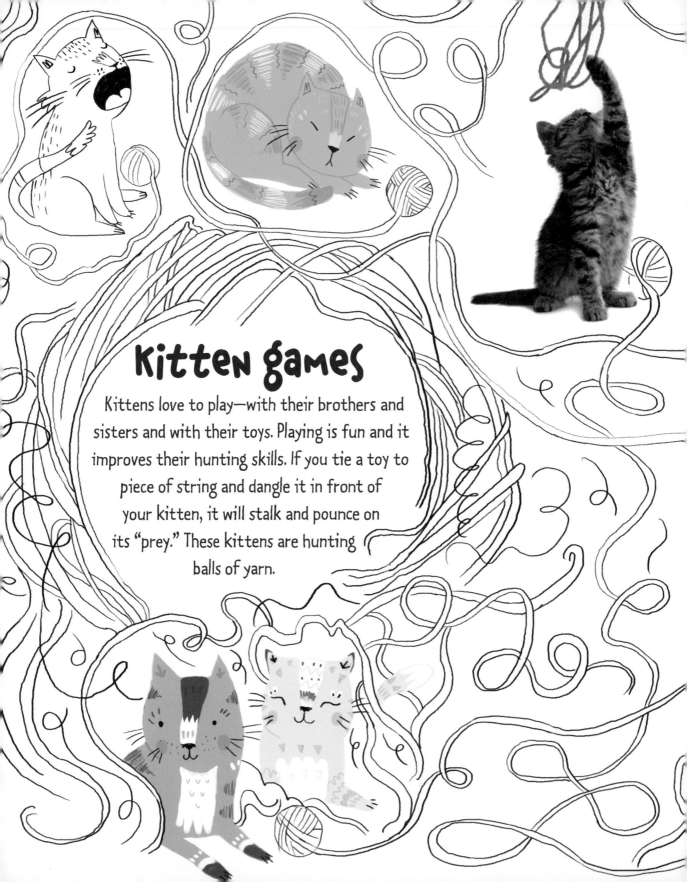

kitten games

Kittens love to play—with their brothers and sisters and with their toys. Playing is fun and it improves their hunting skills. If you tie a toy to piece of string and dangle it in front of your kitten, it will stalk and pounce on its "prey." These kittens are hunting balls of yarn.

CONNECT THE KITTENS TO THEIR PALS.

At 30 days old, kittens can walk, mew, and play.

Kittens are born with their eyes and ears closed.

Blow-up puffer fish

Going about its daily business, a puffer fish looks very ordinary. This makes it seem like easy prey for many bigger fish. But the puffer fish has a trick up its sleeve. It can quickly fill its body with water and turn into a spiked ball that is almost impossible to eat.

Even if a predator manages to swallow a puffer fish, it could be in for a nasty surprise, since some are very poisonous.

DRAW MORE PUFFER FISH PUFFING UP.

Puffer fish will only puff
up if they are threatened!

Some people like to eat puffer fish. A skilled chef prepares the fish so that all the poison is cut away.

DRAW MORE CAMELS WITH ONE OR TWO HUMPS.

Bactrian camels
have two humps.

One hump or two?

Camels live in the desert, and they can go for days without drinking. People once thought it was because they stored water in their humps! This isn't true—the humps are actually filled with fat. But the humps do help camels on long treks, because the fat inside provides the camels with the energy they need.

Dromedary camels have one hump.

High in the Sky!

The sky is full of living creatures. Many birds fly, and some travel long distances from country to country every year. Insects such as butterflies and some beetles fly. In fact, there are billions of insects in the air at any one time. Bats fly, too. They are the only furry animals that do!

Although penguins are birds, they can't fly—unless you give them a jet pack!

FIND THE CREATURE THAT SHOULDN'T BE IN THE AIR. THEN COLOR ALL THE ANIMALS THAT REALLY FLY.

wolf-cub club

When wolf cubs are born, they join a pack of about six or seven other wolves, made up of their own family and a few others. The leader of the pack is always their dad. The other positions in the pack are worked out through fights. Wolf cubs practice fighting by playing and wrestling with the other cubs .

COLOR
THE PLAY-FIGHTING WOLF CUBS.

Wolf cubs stay with their
pack for one to three years
after they are born.

As wolf cubs grow, they start
to eat lumps of meat that
have been softened for them
by other pack members.

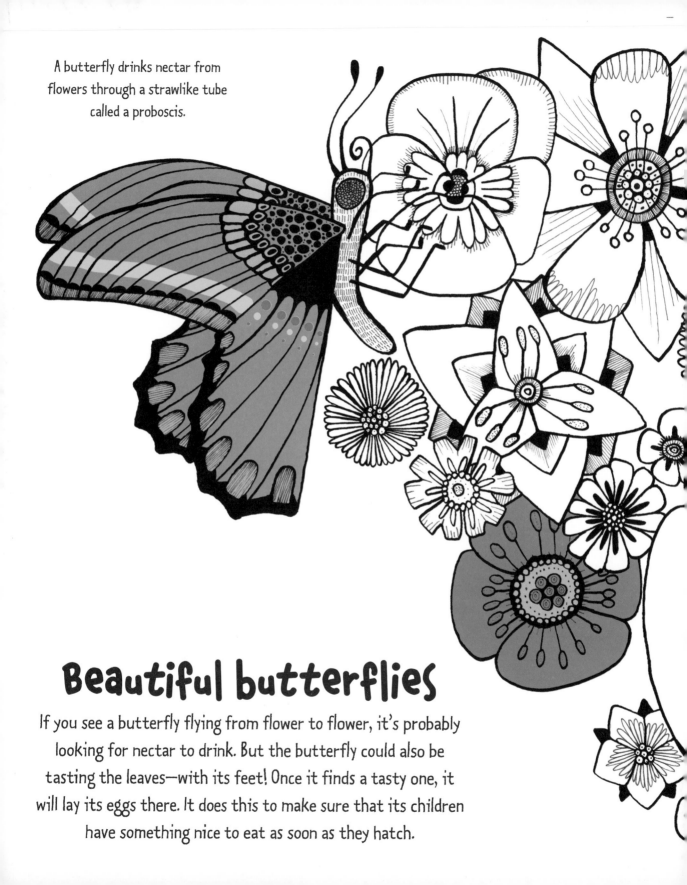

A butterfly drinks nectar from flowers through a strawlike tube called a proboscis.

Beautiful butterflies

If you see a butterfly flying from flower to flower, it's probably looking for nectar to drink. But the butterfly could also be tasting the leaves—with its feet! Once it finds a tasty one, it will lay its eggs there. It does this to make sure that its children have something nice to eat as soon as they hatch.

COLOR THE SCENE AND **DRAW** MORE BUTTERFLIES DRINKING NECTAR.

Butterfly eggs hatch into caterpillars. Later, the caterpillars turn into butterflies.

DRAW MORE SQUIRRELS GLIDING BETWEEN THE TREES.

In the air flying squirrels steer themselves by moving their arms, legs, and tails.

High-flying Squirrels

Is it a bird? Is it a bat? No, it's a flying squirrel! In fact, a flying squirrel doesn't actually fly; it glides. The skin on each side of its body extends from its wrists to its ankles, making a sheet that acts like a parachute. When a squirrel wants to glide down from a tree, it stretches its arms and legs out wide and jumps.

Flying squirrels are expert pilots. They always land safely—even on narrow branches.

Completely cuckoo

Cunning cuckoos trick other birds into raising their young. They lay their eggs in the nests of other birds. They can color their eggs to match those already in the nest so it is harder for the parent bird to notice it.

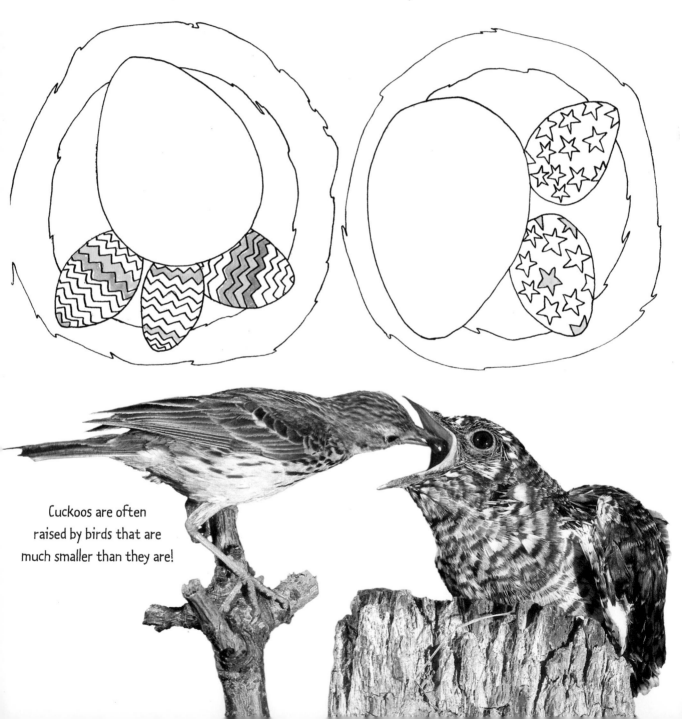

Cuckoos are often raised by birds that are much smaller than they are!

The cuckoo egg is usually much bigger than the eggs already in the nest.

COLOR THE CUCKOO EGG TO MATCH THE EGGS IN THE NEST.

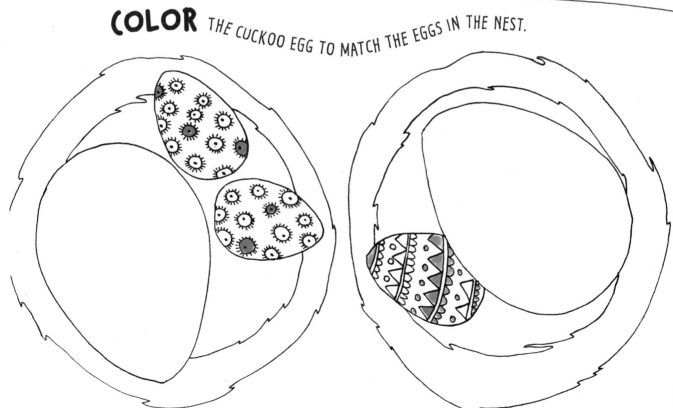

Mole maze

It's a wonder that moles don't get lost in their underground tunnels! Their eyes are small—and it's dark underground—so they can't see very well at all. They also can't hear much either. But their snouts (noses) are long and very sensitive, so they find their way around using their sense of touch.

Moles spend their time underground eating, sleeping, and digging.

HELP THE MOLES FIND THEIR WAY HOME.

Moles eat worms, insects, and grubs
that they find in the tunnels.

DRAW YOUR OWN SAVANNA SCENE.

tiger eyes

It's hard to spot a tiger. They usually sleep during the day and their striped coats help them hide in woodlands and grassy savannas. Their black stripes look like shadows in a sunny landscape.

Tigers are fierce hunters.
They eat small animals like frogs
as well as big ones like antelopes.

Tigers live alone, except for
cubs, who live with their
mothers until they are about
one or two years old.

kangaroo kicks

Kangaroos move around by jumping, using their powerful back legs to travel in big leaps over long distances. Their legs are so strong that the biggest kangaroos can jump up to 40ft (12m) in one bounce. That's farther than the length of two cars!

If a kangaroo could kick a football, it would probably be the best placekicker on the team!

Kangaroo babies are called joeys. They spend the first months of their lives warm and snug in their mother's pouch.

DRAW MORE KANGAROOS JUMPING.

DRAW MORE BEAVERS IN AND AROUND THEIR LODGE.

Beavers' front teeth never stop growing! They don't get too long though, because they are worn down by the wood and bark the beavers gnaw on.

Beavers eat tree bark. In the winter, they store it in the lake, using the water as a refrigerator to keep the bark fresh.

Beaver builders

Beavers are busy builders. They cut down trees with their strong teeth. Then they use the wood to build dams to create a pool of water. They build their lodge (home) in the pool or on its bank. The lodge has a floor above the water and it's very warm and snug. The beavers can get to it from the land as well as from the water.

ADD MORE SIX-SIDED CELLS TO THE HONEYCOMB.

Busy bees

Bees are very useful—they spread pollen from flower to flower while collecting nectar to take back to their hives. There, worker bees change the nectar into honey. The beehive is perfect for storing honey. It's packed with layers of honeycomb made up of thousands of six-sided cells (boxes) for the bees to fill.

Bees live in colonies where everyone has a specific job to do.

DRAW MORE BEES RETURNING TO THE HIVE.

Worker bees also make wax, which they mold into honeycombs.

Gorillas live in family groups of around 10–15 adults and young.

CONNECT THE YOUNG GORILLAS TO THE ADULTS.

Gorilla campsite

Gorillas spend their days traveling through the rainforest. Every night they build new nests where they sleep. Young gorillas and lighter females sleep in trees, while heavier gorillas sleep on the ground.

Gorillas may look scary, but they are actually peaceful plant-eaters.

under the Sea!

The world's oceans are huge! From giant whales to tiny creatures, millions of animals call the sea their home. The oceans are so big and deep that no one knows exactly how many sea creatures there are. There could be hundreds of animals that haven't yet been discovered hiding in the depths!

COLOR IN ALL THE SEA CREATURES.

Crocodile care

Crocodiles are fierce hunters that catch prey in their powerful jaws. You might be surprised to learn that crocodile moms carry their new babies in their jaws, too! But when they do, they're extremely gentle and never close their mouths. The babies are safe between those sharp teeth.

Crocodile babies hatch from their eggs on land, but Mom soon carries them to the water.

Young crocodiles stay with their mothers until they are a few weeks old.

DRAW MORE BABY CROCODILES.

Leap frog!

Ribbit! Frogs are excellent jumpers. They use their powerful back legs to push off, and can jump as much as 40 times their own length. That would be like an adult jumping the length of six buses!

Frogs can change direction quickly between hops. This keeps their enemies on their toes!

DRAW MORE FROGS LEAPING BETWEEN THE LILYPADS.

Frogs are amphibians. This means that they can live both on land and in water.

Ear Signals

Horses can't tell you how they're feeling. But they can show you, if you just look at their ears. When horses are happy and alert, their ears stand straight up. When they're relaxed, their ears are floppy. And when they're feeling angry or grumpy, their ears lie straight back in warning. That's when it's best to steer clear!

ALERT

DRAW MORE HORSES IN THE STABLES.

ANGRY

Horses are very social
animals and like to
live in groups.

DRAW MORE HORSES IN THE FIELD.

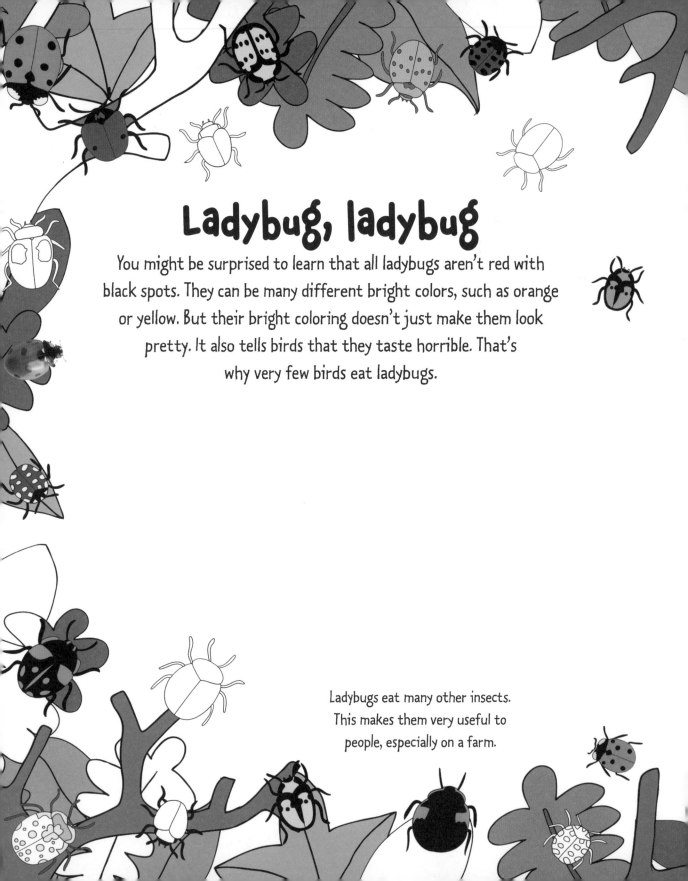

Ladybug, ladybug

You might be surprised to learn that all ladybugs aren't red with black spots. They can be many different bright colors, such as orange or yellow. But their bright coloring doesn't just make them look pretty. It also tells birds that they taste horrible. That's why very few birds eat ladybugs.

Ladybugs eat many other insects. This makes them very useful to people, especially on a farm.

DRAW MORE LADYBUGS AND **COLOR** THEM IN.

Ladybugs sleep through the winter, sometimes snoozing in large groups inside tree trunks or sheds.

Lazy hippo days

Hippos like to spend their days keeping cool in the water. Their eyes, ears, and noses are all on the tops of their heads, so they can stay almost completely underwater, and still be able to see, hear, and breathe.

Hippos can close their nostrils and ears when they dive.

Hippos would rather walk along the bottom of a river than swim—unless you give them a giant rubber inner tube!

I might have sharp teeth and a huge mouth, but I only eat grass!

DRAW MORE HIPPOS STAYING COOL IN THE WATER.

Pigs in mud

Mmm, there's nothing like a mud bath on a hot day! Pigs splash around in muddy water to keep cool, but mud does another job, too. It sticks to their skin and protects the pigs from the Sun's hot rays—kind of like the sunscreen you use when you go to the beach!

DRAW MORE PIGS
ROLLING IN THE MUD.

Being covered in mud also keeps the pigs from being bitten by insects. Yet another reason to jump right in!

Social Sea otters

Sea otters are social creatures. To stay close to their
family and friends, they form floating groups called rafts.
Before they go to sleep, sea otters may wrap themselves
in a seaweed called kelp. The kelp is attached to the
seabed and keeps the otters from drifting away.
Sometimes they even hold each others' paws!

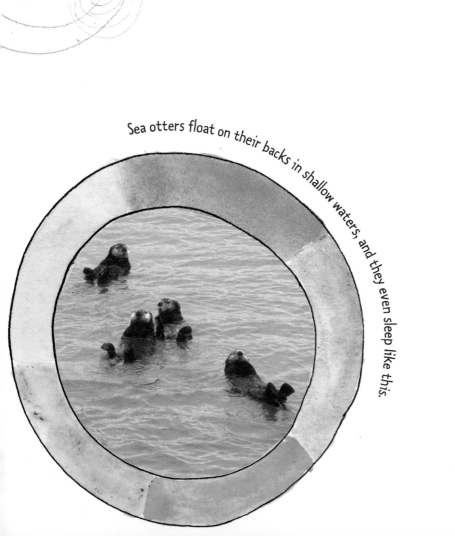

Sea otters float on their backs in shallow waters, and they even sleep like this.

DRAW MORE SEA OTTERS FORMING RAFTS.

Sea otters spend most of their
lives in the water. Their thick fur
helps them stay warm.

In the summer, when the ice melts, polar bears eat whatever they can find. This could be land animals, birds, eggs, and plants—or even garbage left behind by humans!

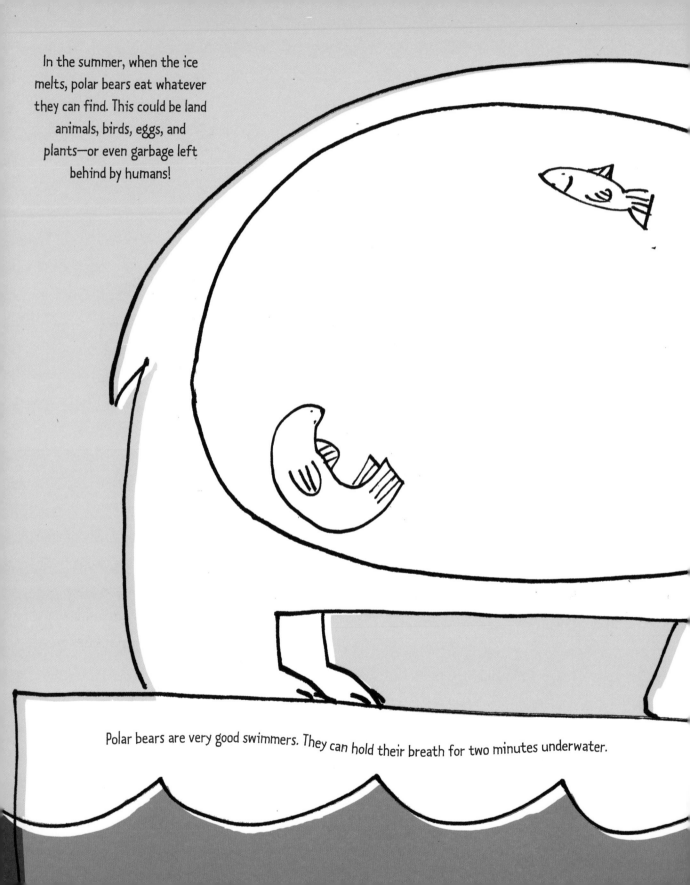

Polar bears are very good swimmers. They can hold their breath for two minutes underwater.

DRAW SOME MORE THINGS THAT THIS POLAR BEAR MAY HAVE EATEN FOR HIS DINNER.

Polar-bear hunt

A polar bear may look cuddly, but it is actually a fierce hunter. It hunts seals that also live on the ice. The polar bear's white coat helps it stay hidden when it follows a seal. If the seal turns around, the polar bear stands very still, and the seal can't see it against the white snow. When the polar bear gets close enough, it quickly snaps up its dinner.

Water spiders eat insects that live in the water. Then they might get eaten by frogs or fish.

Water spiders live in slow-moving water, where their homes won't be washed away.

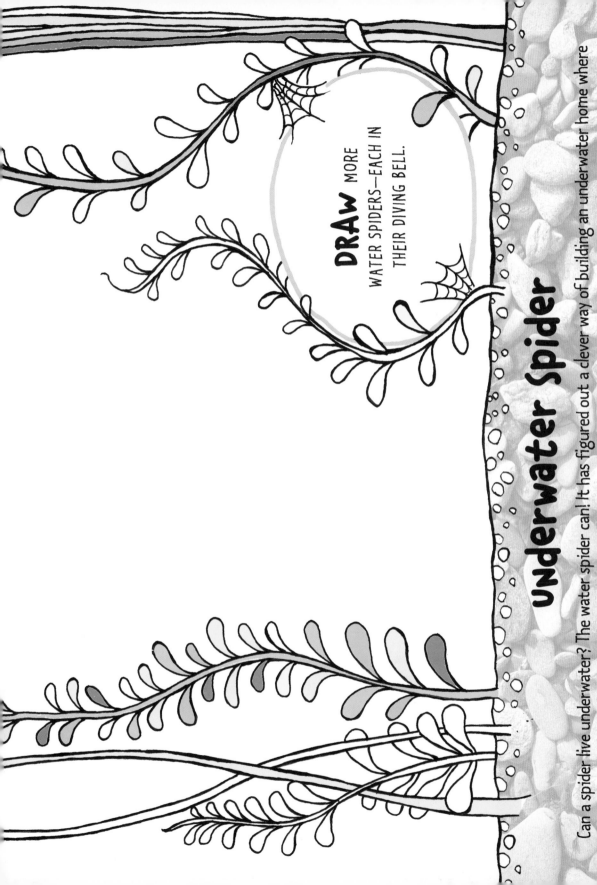

DRAW MORE WATER SPIDERS—EACH IN THEIR DIVING BELL.

underwater Spider

Can a spider live underwater? The water spider can! It has figured out a clever way of building an underwater home where it can breathe. It spins a web underwater and fills it with bubbles of air from the surface that it traps in the hairs on its body. The small bubbles all join up to make a bigger bubble called a diving bell. (Another name for this spider is the diving-bell spider.) The spider lives inside the air-filled diving bell, leaving it only to catch insects and bring down more air bubbles.

When cygnets are small, they're covered in fuzzy gray feathers called down. They don't get their white feathers until they're a little older.

Swan love

Swans are true romantics. When they meet the swan of their dreams, they stay together for years, and sometimes even for life. Together they make a nest that's more than 3ft (1m) wide. Up to eight fuzzy swan babies (called cygnets) hatch to swan couples each spring. The babies stay with their parents until they are around six months old.

DRAW MORE SWANS WITH THEIR CYGNETS.

Cygnets start swimming soon after they hatch. When they get tired, they sometimes hitch a ride on mom's or dad's back!

whale watch

Whales are some of the biggest animals on the planet. It might surprise you to learn that some whales don't eat large animals, but instead eat huge amounts of tiny shrimp called krill. These whales don't have teeth—they filter their food through hairy plates (called baleen plates) that hang down in their mouths. These act like a strainer, only letting in small items of food.

DRAW SOMETHING
FANTASTIC
TO FINISH THE SECTION.

ACKNOWLEDGMENTS

Edited by Alexander Cox, Lorrie Mack, James Mitchem, Laura Palosuo, Lee Wilson, Elizabeth Yeates

Designed by Jess Bentall, Charlotte Bull, Jane Ewart, Anna Formanek, Ria Holland, Charlotte Johnson, Sadie Thomas

Text by Alexander Cox, Elinor Graham, Wendy Horobin, Susan Maylan, James Mitchem,
Ben Morgan, Laura Palosuo, Lee Wilson, Elizabeth Yeates

Fact checker Kim Bryan, Wendy Horobin, Darren Naish

US Editor Margaret Parrish

Illustrators Emma Atkinson, Carolyn Bayley, Evannave, Holly Blackman, Amber Cassidy, Helen Dodsworth, Carly Epworth,
Nic Farrell, Sean Gee, Rob Griffiths, Chris Howker, Barney Ibbotson, Jake McDonald, Peter Todd, Dan Woodger, Jay Wright

PICTURE CREDITS

The publisher would like to thank the following for their kind permission to reproduce their photographs:
(Key: a-above; b-below/bottom; c-center; f-far; l-left; r-right; t-top)

Dorling Kindersley: Jamie Marshall 15r; NASA / JPL 16bl; International Robotics 7ca, 7cra, 101bl;
Lindsey Stock 20cl; Young 42clb; Milo and Snoop 51tl; NASA 56bc; Judith Miller / Freeman's 59tr;
Oxford University Museum of Natural History 59tl; Bethany Dawn 62–63; Stephen Oliver 63ftl;
Natural History Museum, London,73cr; Jamie Marshall 78–79; Royal Armouries 85bl; Josef Hlasek 99bl;
Whipsnade Zoo, Bedfordshire 99cr; Rough Guides 106c, 106l.

All other images © Dorling Kindersley

For further information see: **www.dkimages.com**

GOODBYE!